Perilous Lessons:
The Impact of the WTO Services Agreement (GATS) on Canada's Public Education System

Jim Grieshaber-Otto
and Matt Sanger

Canadian Centre for Policy Alternatives
2002

Copyright © 2002 Canadian Centre for Policy Alternatives and the authors.

All rights reserved. No part of this book may be reproduced or transmitted in any form or by any means, electronic or mechanical, including photocopying, or by any information storage or retrieval system, without permission in writing from the publisher or the author.

National Library of Canada Cataloguing in Publication Data

Grieshaber-Otto, Jim
    Perilous lessons : the impact of the WTO Services Agreement (GATS) on Canada's public education system / Jim Grieshaber-Otto, Matthew Sanger.

Includes bibliographical references.
ISBN 0-88627-273-4

    1. Education and state—Canada. 2. General Agreement on Trade in Services (1994). I. Sanger, Matthew II. Canadian Centre for Policy Alternatives III. Title.

LA412.G75 2002   379.71   C2002-902923-6

Printed and bound in Canada

Published by

Canadian Centre for Policy Alternatives
Suite 410, 75 Albert Street
Ottawa, ON K1P 5E7
Tel 613-563-1341   Fax 613-233-1458
http://www.policyalternatives.ca
ccpa@policyalternatives.ca

We dedicate this book to our parents, for whom the education of subsequent generations is paramount.

Contents

Acknowledgements i

Summary iii

Introduction 1

Chapter 1: The GATS, human rights and Canada's public education system 5
1.1 From the GATT to the WTO 5
1.2 What is the GATS; what are services? 6
1.3 Education services in the GATS 9
1.4 Trade rules and the right to education in international human rights law 11
1.5 The right of choice amidst diversity 18
in education 18

Chapter 2: Coverage of public education in the GATS .. 23
2.1 The GATS covers most public service systems, including education 23
   2.1.1 The GATS is very broad 23
   2.1.2 The GATS "governmental authority" exclusion is unlikely to provide substantive protection for education 24
2.2 What are education services? 29
   2.2.1 What are services? How are they classified? 29
   2.2.2 How are most education services classified in the GATS? 30
   2.2.3 How are other education services, or other services associated with education, classified in the GATS? 31
2.3 Which GATS rules now apply to education? 38
   2.3.1 GATS general rules already apply "across the board" 38
   2.3.2 GATS specific rules, which apply only to listed services 40
   2.3.3 Other GATS provisions 42

Chapter 3: The impact of the current GATS treaty amid the increasing commercialization of education 45

3.1 The context for GATS negotiations: increasing commercialization and privatization of education 46

   3.1.1 Public schools generate commercial revenue 47

   3.1.2 Commercial services operate within public schools 58

   3.1.3 Public funding of private education 62

   3.1.4 Commercial public schools: The emergence of Education Management Organizations (EMOs) 63

3.2 In brief: the impacts of commercialization and privatization 76

3.3 Clash of principles: GATS vs. the public education system 76

   3.3.1 Education policies that are deemed to be "barriers to trade" are targeted in GATS negotiations 77

3.4 Some impacts of the GATS, and of commercialization and privatization, are mutually reinforcing 84

   3.4.1 Increased commercialization and privatization leads to greater GATS coverage, both directly and indirectly. 84

   3.4.2 Increased commercialization and privatization increases domestic pressure for GATS expansion 89

   3.4.3 The GATS exerts unrelenting pressure for greater commercialization and privatization 91

3.5 The GATS – at it now exists – contains specific threats to public education systems 92

   3.5.1 GATS general obligations already apply to education 93

   3.5.2. There are as yet few GATS specific commitments in education-related services 103

Chapter 4: Future threats: Negotiations to expand the GATS 105

4.1 The risks of an ever-expanding treaty 105

4.2 Treaty by stealth? The problems of legal uncertainty and misunderstanding 106

4.3 Unrelenting pressure for new, more extensive GATS specific commitments 108

4.3.1 National treatment 110
4.3.2 Market access 113
4.3.3 Classification issues 115
4.4. Pressure for other GATS concessions 117
4.4.1 GATS negotiations on Domestic Regulation 118

Chapter 5: Canada's approach in the current GATS round 121
5.1 Canada's stated GATS objectives for education: Unsustainable balancing act between conflicting aims? 122
5.2 Poised to make specific commitments affecting education ... 126
5.3 Playing down the risks: Providing unbalanced, misleading information to the public 129
    5.3.1 Assertion: Governments' regulatory ability is protected 130
    5.3.2 Assertion: Canada retains the right to maintain public services 131
    5.3.3 Assertion: Public education is not negotiable 132
    5.3.4 Assertion: GATS does not require privatization or deregulation 133
    5.3.5 Assertion: Canada's public education is protected: Revisiting the 'governmental authority' exclusion 133

Chapter 6: Revising the lesson: Conclusion and recommendations 137
6.1 GATS: Casting a lengthening shadow over education 137
6.2 Reassurances from the federal government: overly optimistic and misleading 141
6.3 Changing Canada's approach to the GATS and education 143
    6.3.1 Specific changes Canada can make unilaterally 145
    6.3.2 Changes in the GATS that Canada must negotiate with other WTO members 146
    6.3.3 Beyond the GATS 148
    6.3.4 Getting started 150

Endnotes 155
Introduction 155
Chapter 1 155
Chapter 2 158
Chapter 3 163
Chapter 4 173
Chapter 5 177
Chapter 6 185

Sidebars
What Is Trade in Services? 7
International Instruments Concerning the Right to Education 13
International classification of "education services" 32
Education related services that fall outside the "education services" category 37
Wal-Mart "adopts" schools 52
Canadian Education Centre Networks 54
Examining Edison Schools, Inc. – 66
United States: Education "obstacles" for review in GATS negotiations 82

Acknowledgements

The authors wish to thank Diana Bronson, Mark Ciavaglia, Cynthia Callard, Bruce Campbell, Diane Exley, Ed Finn, Kerri-Anne Finn, Ellen Gould, Emil and Mary Otto Grieshaber, Severin Iseli, Sabina Iseli-Otto, Larry Kuehn, Patricia McAdie, Brendan McCombs, Mary O'Neill, Karen Philp, Susan Robertson, Carole Samdup, Noel Schacter and other members of the CCPA Trade and Investment Research Project for their invaluable suggestions, comments and other support. We are particularly grateful to Scott Sinclair, who helped see it through from start to finish. We are also very grateful to the many organizations that made this book possible by providing financial assistance to the Trade and Investment Research Project. The inspiring efforts of a growing number of researchers, organizations and citizens around the world are also gratefully acknowledged. Finally, we thank our friends and especially our families for their unstinting support, encouragement, and generosity of spirit during the duration of this project.

Summary

The General Agreement on Trade in Services (GATS)—a global treaty on services—already threatens to erode Canada's public education system. Canada's approach in the current round of negotiations to expand the treaty could worsen existing threats, and subsequent rounds will pose even more serious hazards to public education in the future. While not likely to bring about immediate changes, the GATS reinforces commercializing forces already at work in the education system and, if unattended, could foreclose vital policy options. Fortunately, the GATS and negotiations underway to expand it are finally beginning to attract the public attention and scrutiny they deserve. To protect the future of public education in Canada, it is essential that citizens and public education advocates across the country become actively involved now in the critical GATS debate.

> **GATS coverage of education**
>
> The GATS covers all types of actions taken by governments and school boards that "affect" trade in education services, and all the ways in which these services are supplied, including electronically. In principle, the treaty covers all services that comprise the public education system even though these may not formally be classified as "education services". Its coverage is thus not limited to classroom teaching, but extends to library services, counseling services, tutoring, student testing, and speech therapy. It also covers teacher recruitment, secretarial services, records keeping, grounds keeping, school management, and even pension fund administration and labour union services.

Almost unknown to the general public, the GATS is an extraordinarily ambitious agreement. It is exceptionally broad in scope, and the treaty's legally enforceable obligations are backed up by trade sanctions. The GATS contains some general rules that apply across-the-board to government regulation of education at the federal, provincial, and local school board level. The treaty also contains more onerous specific rules, which apply only to sectors specified by individual members, and which do not yet apply to most aspects of the education system. However, this could change as, critically, the GATS contains a built-in commitment to repeated re-negotiations to expand its coverage.

GATS rules

The GATS general rules already apply 'across the board' to all education services.

- The GATS <u>Most-Favoured Nation</u> (MFN) obligation requires that the best treatment accorded to *any* foreign service provider must be accorded "immediately and unconditionally" to *all* foreign service providers. This obligation has the practical effect of consolidating any commercialization, privatization or other market-opening measures involving foreign service providers.

- The GATS <u>transparency</u> rules require members to publish all existing measures, at all levels of government, that "pertain to or affect the operation" of the treaty. Seemingly benign, these rules entail new administrative demands that may be particularly onerous for local school boards and provincial governments that administer education systems. These reporting requirements are also a means to target education measures for further liberalization in subsequent negotiating rounds.

The GATS specific rules apply only to listed services. These powerful provisions apply only to those sectors where a

---

member has undertaken specific commitments. Canada and most other countries have not yet agreed to apply these rules to education and the education sector is currently among the most "uncommitted."

- The GATS <u>national treatment</u> rule requires members to extend the best treatment that is given domestically to foreign services and suppliers. Broader than generally recognized, this non-discrimination provision requires that every advantage given to a domestic service or service provider must be accorded to a like foreign service or service provider.
- The GATS rules on <u>market access</u> prohibit certain numerical limits on services or suppliers; they are absolute, preventing such limits outright even if they do not discriminate against foreign services or suppliers.

The GATS contains other rules, including:
- <u>Domestic regulation</u>. Negotiations are currently underway to develop "disciplines" to ensure that government measures do not constitute "unnecessary barriers to trade in services."

The aims of the GATS conflict with the basic principles underlying public education.

Clash of principles

The principles of the GATS are, at root, in conflict with those of Canada's public education system. The impetus of the GATS is to expand commercial opportunities for foreign service providers and investors—in short, to commercialize services. Canada's public education system exists to ensure free, high-quality education for all regardless of citizens' financial circumstances or their ability to pay.

The GATS also exerts constant pressure for privatization and commercialization, and consolidates this trend wherever it occurs. In turn, increased commercialization leads—directly and indirectly—to greater GATS coverage. In other words, steadily increasing commercial pressures, which already exist independently of the GATS, reinforce the effects of the treaty and, in turn, are reinforced by it. These mutually reinforcing effects are especially important in light of the many commercial activities that already occur in and around schools. They are also increasingly relevant following the recent proliferation, in the United States, of so-called Education Management Organizations (EMOs)—private firms that manage <u>public</u> schools for profit.

Even though the impacts of the existing treaty, which was adopted in 1994, have not been adequately assessed, negotiations are currently underway to expand its reach. Barring a fundamental change in the direction of these negotiations, new and more onerous provisions affecting education are likely, through:

- more extensive GATS specific commitments involving national treatment and market access,
- the application of GATS rules to an increasing number of so-called "ancillary" aspects of the public education system,
- new constraints on domestic regulation, including a test of regulatory "necessity," affecting qualification requirements, technical standards and licensing procedures.

These negotiations could extend the reach of the treaty into the very heart of governments' regulatory authority over public education.

> ### The GATS "governmental authority" exclusion
> Contrary to common understanding and repeated suggestions by proponents, the GATS contains no general exclusion for public services, and the exclusion that does exist—for "services supplied in the exercise of governmental authority"—is unclear, narrow and will be interpreted restrictively. It is likely to provide little or no substantive protection for public education.

Canada maintains that the country's public education system will not be put at risk in the current round of GATS negotiations. The federal government has not yet applied the toughest GATS rules to the most important aspects of public education in Canada. However, Canada is an active proponent of continuous GATS expansion, and the evidence indicates that the federal government is poised to make specific treaty commitments affecting domestic public education. **Whether blithely, or knowingly and recklessly, the federal government seems to be taking an approach to GATS negotiations that could exacerbate threats that the treaty already poses to Canada's K-12 public education system.** Meanwhile, federal representatives repeatedly play down the risks of the treaty and provide unbalanced, and sometimes misleading, information to the public.

A radical shift in Canada's approach to education in the GATS – and to the GATS itself – is urgently required.

Fortunately, a dramatic shift in trade policy is feasible. Canada still retains a significant degree of policy flexibility, and a variety of practical means, to address citizens' priorities for education in the international realm. Canada could unilaterally make a number of changes to its approach to GATS and education. For example:

- Canada should adopt a precautionary approach and seek to "do no harm" to its vital public education system in the current and any future GATS negotiations;
- Canada should make no GATS commitments in any education-related sectors (either public or private);
- Canada should not seek any education-related GATS commitments from other countries;
- Federal, provincial and territorial governments should conduct a thorough assessment of the implications of Canada's existing commitments affecting education before Canada makes any further GATS proposals.

Canada can also negotiate with other GATS members to effect other changes. For example:
- Canada should support a thorough assessment of trade in services at the GATS, and support Southern country demands that an initial assessment be concluded before further negotiations proceed;
- Canada should propose a general, "horizontal" exception for all measures affecting education;
- Canada should mount a serious negotiating effort to ensure that no so-called "disciplines" are developed in the GATS negotiations on domestic regulation;
- Canada should insist on changes to the "governmental authority" exclusion so that its meaning is clarified, and, critically, that it is made fully effective.

None of these things will occur by themselves. Canadians – whether parents, teachers, board members, administrators, students, researchers, or others involved in education; or ordinary citizens—must therefore become actively involved in the GATS debate to ensure that these things do occur. As a practical prerequisite for achieving progress in countering the many GATS threats to education, it will be necessary for public education advocates to overcome an understandable sense of disbelief. It is difficult to grasp—both intellectually and emotionally—the full scope of the GATS and its impacts, and the significance of what is being proposed in Geneva. But it is only a matter of time before a significant number of citizens throughout the world realize just how far, and in what direction, GATS negotiators have been allowed to proceed. At that juncture, citizens will be in a position to begin seriously to engage on the threats posed by the treaty and to ensure that fundamental changes are made.

There are significant grounds for optimism showing that the efforts of well-organized groups of concerned citizens can have real influence in international negotiations—not just on the specifics of a particular treaty, but on the fate of treaties themselves.

> **The influence of well-organized concerned citizens**
> "In late 1998 the proposed Multilateral Agreement on Investment (MAI), an agreement that shared the GATS excessive reach and whose proponents exhibited a similar overweening ambition, suffered a stunningly unexpected defeat largely at the hands of a well-informed, sophisticated and organized international citizenry."

Several significant deadlines are approaching:
- June 30, 2002 is the deadline for Canada to make initial requests of other countries, and for Canada to receive other countries' initial requests for market openings in our education service sector,
- March 31, 2003 is the deadline for Canada, and other countries, to make initial offers to expand the reach of the GATS by making additional specific commitments under the treaty,

- January 1, 2005 is the deadline to conclude the current round of WTO negotiations, including those to expand the GATS.

The active involvement in the GATS debate by public education advocates throughout Canada—in every community and school district, and in every province and territory—is as urgent as it is critical.

Introduction

These are difficult and ominous times for public education in Canada. They will become even more troubling if international trade rules place limits on the ability of citizens, through their governments and school authorities, to determine the future of our children's schools.

What is the GATS—the General Agreement on Trade in Services? Why should anyone care? Why have most people never heard of it? Do its global rules apply to Canada's public education system? Does it affect education in Canada? In every province? If so, how? Could it affect local school boards? Will it compromise Canada's ability to put the public interest first when governments and local education authorities address crucial issues that already face public education? Will the treaty help Canadian education businesses operating overseas? What role has the Canadian government played in the negotiations that are now underway in Geneva to expand the GATS? Finally, what should be done? How can Canadians—and the education-related organizations to which they belong—become actively involved in the critical issues that are on the GATS negotiating table?

The purpose of this report is to examine the implications of the GATS—and of GATS negotiations now underway in Geneva—for Canada's public education system. In addressing the above questions, it raises worrisome concerns about Canada's approach in the GATS negotiations, and the possible consequences for primary and secondary level education.

PART I
The GATS and education:
What's all the fuss about?[1]

The report begins, in **Chapter 1**, with an introduction to the GATS. Its point of departure is the right of citizens to education that is contained in long-standing and well-established international human rights law. The section discusses the general significance of these rights and of the GATS in the context of recent education policy initiatives.

Chapter 2 examines the existing GATS treaty and considers whether it covers our public education system. It considers how education and related services are classified in the treaty, and which of the GATS rules now apply to this sector.

Chapter 3 considers the current trends towards increased commercialization and privatization, providing examples of various forms of each. It discusses how these effects may interact with, and amplify, the effects of the GATS. It also highlights some of the ways in which the existing treaty already threatens public education.

PART II
The Devil's in the detail

Chapter 4 employs numerous illustrative hypothetical examples to describe the threats that future negotiations on an ever-expanding treaty are likely to pose for Canada's public education system.

Chapter 5 examines Canada's approach to the current round of GATS re-negotiation. It describes Canada's conflicting GATS objectives for education and how federal representatives consistently play down the treaty's domestic risks as Canada proceeds down an increasingly hazardous one-way street.

PART III Where do we go from here?

Chapter 6, which concludes the study, offers specific recommendations to individuals and organizations seeking to reduce and/or eliminate the GATS threats in order to build a more balanced future for Canada's vital public education system.

Chapter 1
The GATS, human rights and Canada's public education system

Assessing the implications of the GATS for public education is a challenge. The GATS is a complex treaty, and an examination must take into account its untested provisions and its ambitious agenda of further liberalization. An examination must also consider the regulatory framework of the sector, its administrative arrangements, and the enormous pressure public education faces to deliver more with less funding.

This chapter sets the stage for a more detailed analysis contained in the chapters that follow. It introduces the broad parameters of the GATS and then briefly reviews potential conflicts between the GATS and international human rights obligations.

1.1 From the GATT to the WTO

In 1995, after eight years of complex negotiations, the World Trade Organization—commonly known as the WTO—came into being. The WTO marked a fundamental change in the multilateral trading regime, which until then had been presided over by the General Agreement on Tariffs and Trade (GATT). The GATT was an international agreement among contracting parties that focused primarily on reducing tariffs and other at-the-border trade restrictions on the trade of goods.

Under the GATT system, governments had the option to choose which side agreements they wished to adhere to. The GATT dispute settlement process was basically diplomatic; that is, its rulings were adopted by consensus requiring the agreement even of the government against which a complaint had been brought.

The WTO stands in sharp contrast to the GATT. It is a full-fledged multilateral institution having a far broader scope. Its rules are not limited to trade in goods, but apply to standards, intellectual property, and services. WTO rules are not limited to border measures, but reach into the heart of governments' regulatory authority. Member governments cannot pick and choose between its various agreements; they are bound by all WTO agreements. And, critically, the WTO dispute settlement system is mandatory and legally binding on members, and rulings are backed up by the possibility of punitive trade sanctions.

1.2 What is the GATS; what are services?

The GATS—or the General Agreement on Trade in Services—is a global treaty on services. It is one of a package of treaties that comprises the World Trade Organization. The GATS has been described as "perhaps the most important single development in the multilateral system since the GATT itself came into effect in 1948."[1] Despite its importance, however, the GATS received little attention when the WTO was formed, and has only recently begun to attract significant amounts of public attention.

The subject matter of the GATS—services—is almost unimaginably broad. Services "underpin all forms of international trade and all aspects of global economic activity".[2] Services affect nearly all aspects of our lives. As one analysis[3] has put it:

"Services range from birth (midwifery) to death (burial); the trivial (shoe-shining) to the critical (heart surgery); the personal (hair-cutting) to the social (primary education); low-tech (household

What Is Trade in Services?

The GATS definition of trade in services extends far beyond the common understanding of trade as an exchange across national borders. In the GATS definition, trade in services pertains to all of the various ways in which services are supplied. These so-called "modes of supply" include:

1. <u>Cross-border supply</u>. This mode includes any service provided from the territory of one country into the territory of another country. Examples include mail and mail-order services, telecommunications, Internet, e-commerce businesses, and many financial services. The provision of health and education services through the Internet are a rapidly growing form of cross-border trade.

2. <u>Consumption abroad</u>. In this mode, service consumers (not the service) cross national boundaries. Examples include tourism, students studying abroad and individuals seeking medical treatment in another country.

3. <u>Commercial presence</u>. This mode of service supply includes all foreign direct investment in services providers. Examples include Canadian universities with international operations and U.S. test-preparation companies operating franchises in Canada. The incorporation of this mode into the GATS effectively makes the treaty an investment rights agreement as much as a services or trade agreement.

4. <u>Presence of natural persons</u>. In this mode, individuals travel to another country to provide a service on a temporary basis. This applies most commonly to company managers, technicians, professionals, and consultants whose work involves working abroad.

help) to high-tech (satellite communications); and from our wants (retail sales of toys) to our needs (water distribution)."

The same analysis also notes that
"no government action, whatever its purpose—protecting the environment, safeguarding consumers, enforcing labour standards, promoting fair competition, ensuring universal service, or any other end—is, in principle, beyond GATS scrutiny and potential challenge."

There is no question that primary education is a service to which certain GATS rules apply. However, as will become clear later in this report, the chief task in ascertaining its potential impact is to determine which education services are covered by which GATS rules.

The architecture of the GATS is more complex than most international treaties. The agreement is often described as a "bottom up" treaty, that is, a treaty containing rules that apply only to those service sectors and government measures that WTO member countries agree to list. However, a serious examination reveals that the GATS is a hybrid agreement, containing both "bottom up" rules and rules that apply from the "top down," or universally, to all measures.[4]

Significantly, the GATS contains an overarching requirement for each WTO member to participate in successive rounds of negotiations to expand the reach of the treaty. This built-in feature of the GATS is highly unusual and highlights the importance of not confining an analysis of its effects to a country's present-day commitments. Instead, it is important that such an analysis take into account the fact that the treaty is dynamic, explicitly designed for continuous expansion.

1.3 Education services in the GATS

Nearly 30 WTO members have made commitments under the GATS in primary and secondary education services, although Canada has so far not done so. While education is to date one of the sectors for which the fewest GATS commitments have been made, a number of countries appear to be interested in "liberalizing" various aspects of the sector; these include the EU members, New Zealand, Australia, the United States, Japan, and Mexico. The United States has not made specific GATS commitments in primary and secondary education, but has made commitments in the adult education and training categories and in "other" education services; *see sidebar*.

To date, only the United States, New Zealand, and Australia have proposed extending GATS coverage of education services. As we shall see, the aim is for this to be achieved, in part, through the reduction or elimination of so-called "obstacles" to trade in education services—among which are measures that would widely be considered key aspects of national education policies.

Canada maintains that, while it intends to seek increased access to international markets for Canadian exports of education and training services during this round of GATS re-negotiations, Canada's public education "is not negotiable". In carefully chosen language, Canadian government representatives endeavor to distinguish between commercial and public education, and continue to commit publicly to keep the latter out of the GATS negotiations. As will be considered later in this report, the conflicting nature of the Canadian government's stated ob-

GATS Commitments in Education Services – Selected Countries

Countries	Primary	Secondary	Higher	Adult	Other
Canada (no commitments)					
EC (12 countries)	X	X	X	X	
Japan	X	X	X	X	
Mexico	X	X	X		X
New Zealand	X	X	X		
USA				X	X
Total countries with commitments	32	23	21	20	12

Source: WTO Council for Trade in Services, Education Service – Background Note by the Secretariat (S/C/W/49) 23 September 1998, table 5.

jectives makes it difficult to comprehend how long their balancing act between expanding export opportunities, while also protecting the integrity of public education, can be sustained through repeated rounds of protracted and complex negotiations.

1.4 Trade rules and the right to education in international human rights law

In focusing on the potential impact of the GATS on education, it is easy to overlook the fact that other international treaties also apply to education. Education is recognized as a human right under international human rights law. However, GATS and other trade rules affecting national education policies have been developed seemingly without reference to these human rights laws. Conflicts between the two seem almost certain to emerge, especially given the planned continuous expansion of the GATS. It is therefore important at the outset to examine the relationship between trade and human rights law in some detail.

There is a growing appreciation that treaties such as the GATS must not be viewed in isolation. Two eminent scholars recently concluded that:

"In the event of a conflict between a universally recognized human right and a commitment ensuing from international treaty law such as a trade agreement, the latter must be interpreted to be consistent with the former. When properly interpreted and applied, the trade regime recognizes that human rights are fundamental and prior to free trade itself.[5]

Even in those instances where human rights obligations do not take primacy, the Vienna Convention on the Law of Treaties[6] stipulates, as a general rule, that relevant rules of other international law "shall be taken into account" in the interpretation of treaties such as the WTO. Unfortunately, despite these formal obligations, fundamental human rights appear to receive scant attention in WTO deliberations.[7]

As a member of the global community, Canada has actively promoted international recognition of education as a fundamental human right. Canada played an important role in drafting the Universal Declaration of Human Rights (UDHR), which was adopted in 1948. It declares: "[e]veryone has the right to education" and that [e]ducation shall be free" at the elementary and fundamental levels, "generally available" at the technical and professional levels, and "equally accessible to all on the basis of merit" at the higher level. (*See sidebar.*) Article 26 of the UDHR further stipulates that

"Education shall be directed to the full development of the human personality and the sense of its dignity, and to the strengthening of respect for human rights and fundamental freedoms."

Recognition of this right to education confers obligations on national governments to respect, protect, and fulfill the right to education. In the eyes of international law, these obligations must be taken into account in the interpretation of other treaties, including trade agreements. Moreover, to the extent that they have acquired the status of so-called pre-emptory norms, custom or general principles, human rights—including those relating to education—should have primacy over trade agreements.[8]

International Instruments Concerning the Right to Education

Universal Declaration of Human Rights (UDHR), 1948

Article 26
5. Everyone has the right to education. Education shall be free, at least in the elementary and fundamental stages. Elementary education shall be compulsory. Technical and professional education shall be made generally available and higher education shall be equally accessible to all on the basis of merit.

6. Education shall be directed to the full development of the human personality and the strengthening of respect for human rights and fundamental freedoms. It shall promote understanding, tolerance, and friendship among all nations, racial or religious groups, and shall further the activities of the United Nations for the maintenance of peace.

7. Parents shall have a prior right to choose the kind of education that shall be given to their children.

International Covenant on Economic Social and Cultural Rights (ICESCR), 1966

Article 13
8. The States Parties to the present Covenant recognize the right of everyone to education. They agree that education shall be directed to the full development of the human personality and the sense of its dignity, and shall strengthen the respect for human rights and fundamental freedoms. They further agree that education shall enable all persons to participate effectively in a free society, promote understanding, tolerance, and friendship among all nations and all racial, ethnic, or religious groups, and

further the activities of the United Nations for the maintenance of peace.

9. The States Parties to the present Covenant recognize that, with a view to achieving the full realization of this right:
a. Primary education shall be compulsory and freely available to all;
b. Secondary education in its different forms, including technical and vocational secondary education, shall be made generally available and accessible to all by every appropriate means, and in particular by the progressive introduciton of free education.
c. Higher education shall be made equally accessible to all, on the basis of capacity, by every appropriate means, and in particular by the progressive introduction of free education.
d. Fundamental education shall be encouraged or intensified as far as possible for those persons who have not received or completed the whole period of their primary education.
e. The development of a system of schools at all levels shall be pursued, and adequate fellowship system shall be established, and the material conditions of teaching staff shall be continuously improved.

10. The States Parties to the Present Covenant undertake to have respect for the liberty of parents and, when applicable, legal guardians to choose for their children schools, other than those established by the public authorities, which conform to such minimum educational standards as my be laid down or approved by the State and to ensure the religious and moral education of their children in conformity with their own convictions.

No part of this Article shall be construed so as to interfere with the liberty of individuals and bodies.

What national governments are obliged to do in order to realize the right to education is elaborated in the International Covenant on Economic, Social and Cultural Rights (ICESCR), to which Canada was a founding signatory in 1966, but to which it did not formally accede until 10 years later. Today, Canadians await the decision of the Supreme Court of Canada in the Gosselin vs. Quebec appeal[9] to see whether, or to what extent, the social and economic rights under this Covenant are acknowledged in Canada.

Article 13 of the Covenant stipulates that, in addition to free and compulsory *primary* education, the realization of the right to education requires that *secondary* education "shall be made generally available and accessible to all by every appropriate means, and in particular by progressive introduction of free education."[10]

The responsible UN committee, composed of national government representatives, occasionally issues its deliberations regarding the governmental actions required to implement the various rights set out in the Covenant. Its most recent comment on the right to education amplifies what is meant by the obligation to ensure that secondary schooling is "generally available":

"The phrase 'generally available' signifies, firstly, that secondary schooling is not dependent on a student's apparent capacity or ability and, secondly, that secondary education will be distributed throughout the State in such a way that it is available on the same basis to all."[11]

The committee also sets out the essential features that should characterize education "in all its forms and at all levels":

a. Availability—functioning educational institutions and programmes have to be available in sufficient quantity within the jurisdiction of the State party.
b. Accessibility—educational institutions and programmes have to be accessible to everyone, without discrimination, within the jurisdiction of the State party. Accessibility has three overlapping dimensions:
   - Non-discrimination—education has to be accessible to all, especially the most vulnerable groups, in law and in fact, without discrimination on any of the prohibited grounds.
   - Physical accessibility—education has to be within safe physical reach.
   - Economic accessibility—education has to be affordable to all.
c. Acceptability—the form and substance of education, including curricula and teaching methods, have to be acceptable (e.g., relevant, culturally appropriate, and of good quality) to students and, in appropriate cases, parents.
d. Adaptability—education has to be flexible so it can adapt to the needs of changing societies and communities and respond to the needs of students within their diverse social and cultural settings.[12]

While the obligations of national governments must be interpreted flexibly to ensure that nations with vastly different resources and capabilities are able to realize the right to education, the UN committee is very clear that all national governments are obliged not to erode progress that has been achieved toward its realization.

"There is a strong presumption of impermissibility of any retrogressive measures taken in relation to the right to education, as well as any other rights enunciated in the Covenant. If any deliberately retrogressive measures are taken, the State party has the burden of proving that they have been introduced after the most careful consideration of all alternatives and that they are fully justified by reference to the totality of the rights provided for in the Covenant and in the context of the full use of the State party's maximum available resources."[13]

As well as respecting the right to education in their own direct actions, national governments are obliged to use their influence over corporations and other "third parties" to protect the right to education. "The obligation to protect requires States to take measures that prevent third parties from interfering with the enjoyment of the right to education."[14]

In other words, governments are required to use their available powers to prevent private sector activity that detracts from the right to education. Evidently, government policies that have the opposite effect—for instance, if deregulation and privatization reduces access to education—would be in violation of Canada's international human rights obligations.

National government obligations under the Covenant also extend to their international relations, including participation in trade agreements.

"In relation to the negotiation and ratification of international agreements, States parties should take steps to ensure that these instruments do not adversely impact upon the right to education. Similarly, States parties have an obligation to ensure that their actions as members of international organizations, including international financial institutions, take due account of the right to education."[15]

Canada's international human rights commitments thus include significant and specific obligations regarding the right to education. Yet there is no indication that these obligations are being given the weight they deserve as Canada develops its GATS negotiating position.

In fact, in practical terms, WTO trade rules are likely to take precedence over international human rights. In contrast with WTO obligations, human rights obligations are only weakly enforced. Canada and other nations submit biennnial reports to the Committee, which also invites submissions by non-governmental organizations with an interest in Canada's human rights performance. The committee publicly issues its findings, and has recently chastised Canada for contravention of the Convention. However, the UN Committee has no means to enforce any remedial action on national governments. By contrast, WTO rules are enforced by means of an effective and expeditious dispute settlement process. This glaring imbalance in our system of international law almost guarantees that, in practice, the right to education will be trumped by any conflicting trade rules.[16]

1.5 The right of choice amidst diversity in education

Canadians are fortunate to have a recognized right to universal education that is also a well-established reality. However, due to our federal constitution, Canada also has 13 discrete public education systems, and is the only OECD country without a federal ministry responsible for education.

The Canadian Constitution Act of 1867 recognizes that provinces and territories have exclusive jurisdiction over primary and secondary education, other than schooling for Aboriginal peoples and the children of diplomats and armed forces personnel. In a compromise crucial to Confederation, the provinces recognized the federal responsibility to ensure that provincial governments did not discriminate against schools operated by English or French, Protestant or Catholic minorities. This principle was reaffirmed in the Canadian Charter of Rights and Freedoms (1982), which recognizes the right of English- and French-speaking minorities to school instruction in the minority language, "where numbers warrant."

This decentralized character of public education in Canada has accommodated regional and cultural differences. The issue of minority religious education, and the historical compromise agreed to accommodate it, has, however, also proved challenging for provincial governments.

Provincial governments have taken different approaches to balancing their responsibility to provide free public education for everyone with the recognition given to specific minority education rights in the Constitution Act of 1867. Publicly-funded school boards, defined by linguistic and religious identity, reflected the dominant cultural composition of the provinces at the time of confederation. Public funding for Christian religious schools gradually became anomalous as Canadian society became more diverse and Canada, consistent with international human rights law, recognized the principle of equality for all minority religious groups.

Quebec resolved its historical discrepancy in 1997 by replacing Catholic and Protestant school boards with French and English boards. (Québec, which has the high-

Public Schools and Publicly Funded Private Schools, by Province and Territory

	Public school systems	Publicly funded private schooling
Newfoundland	10 non-denominational boards and 1 province-wide francophone board fully funded from provincial government revenue	None
Prince Edward Island	3 regional school boards, no separate school system funded from provincial revenue plus a uniform provincial property tax	None
Nova Scotia	7 school boards, 6 regional boards and 1 francophone-Acadian board financed from provincial and municipal government revenues federal responsibility for Aboriginal education was transferred to Mi'kmaq reserve communities, which administer schools through a provincial council	None
New Brunswick	Dual English and French systems, each with a single province-wide board. Schools are administered through 12 anglophone and 6 francophone districts. Full provincial funding for public education.	None
Quebec	Separate English- and French-language school boards, 72 in total. Funded from provincial revenue.	Funding for designated private schools of about $3,200 per student (50% of public school grants).
Ontario	72 district school boards, including 12 francophone district boards. 37 school authorities responsible for isolated and hospital schools. Funded by a combination of provincial revenue and local property taxes (with uniform rates set by the province)	None. Proposed income tax credit would subsidize students' private school tuition, rising from 10%/$700 in 2002 to 50%/$3,500 by 2006. Cost estimated at $300 million by 2006.
Manitoba	56 local school boards No separate system or linguistic boards Funded from provincial revenue, including a provincial property tax.	Provincial funding to private schools which implement the provincial curriculum, hire certified teachers and meet other criteria. Some public services shared with private schools.
Saskatchewan	118 school divisions: 88 public, 22 Roman Catholic, 8 francophone Public and separate divisions are funded from provincial revenue and a local property tax. Francophone divisions do not have access to local property taxes, and receive federal as well as provincial grants.	Provincial funding for students at some private vocational schools.

est rate of private school attendance, provides a generous public subsidy to private schools, including private religious schools.) In the same year, Newfoundland abolished denominational boards, replacing them with a single secular system. Alberta publicly funds separate Catholic school

Alberta	69 school authorities: 41 public, 16 separate (15 Catholic, 1 Protestant), 3 francophone, and 9 charter schools Funded equally from provincial government revenue and a pooled property tax fund. (Separate schools can opt out of pooled system and collect property taxes only from local residents.)	Provincial support for private schools which employ certified teachers and teach an approved curriculum. Support was $2,433 per student (60% of basic instruction grant for public schools).
British Columbia	59 local school boards and 1 francophone education authority. Funded from provincial revenue and a pooled property tax.	About 300 private schools receive public funding from the province. Private schools receive a per pupil grant based on the operating costs of local public schools.
Yukon	28 public schools administered by the territorial Department of Education. A French language school board was established in 1996. Fully funded from territorial government revenue.	None
Northwest Territories	32 school divisions, including both public and separate (Roman Catholic) systems in Yellowknife. Yellowknife schools funded partially by a local property tax. Outside Yellowknife all schools fully funded from territorial government revenue.	None
Nunavut		
Source: Canadian Tax Foundation, *Finances of the Nation 1999*, chapter 10.		

authorities, but provides a per-student grant to private schools, including other religious schools. British Columbia has no denominational school boards, but it also provides a per-student grant to private schools, including religious schools, in part to accommodate Doukabours, Sikhs, and other linguistic and religious elements in a diverse population.

By contrast, Ontario has long funded the separate Catholic system fully, while providing no funding to other religious schools. This situation gave rise to a human rights challenge that dovetailed with the Ontario government's desire to further privatize education. Instead of accommodating all faiths within the public system, as was done in other provinces, the Ontario government recently passed legislation extending public funding to all private schools, including religious schools of all faiths.[17]

International human rights law did not require Ontario to take such action. The UDHR[18] recognizes that all parents have a right to choose the kind of education their children receive. This right to choose is further elaborated in the ICESCR[19], which recognizes the right of everyone to establish independent schools as well as the right of parents to choose them for their children. However, there is no obligation in international human rights law for Ontario to extend funding to all private religious schools. The human rights obligation is simply to allow their establishment and to avoid discriminating between faiths:

"...A State party has no obligation to fund institutions established in according with article 13(3) and (4); however, if a State elects to make a financial contribution to private educational institutions, it must do so without discrimination on any of the prohibited grounds."[20]

Canadian and international recognition of minority education rights thereby provided a convenient pretext for the province of Ontario to implement the most sweeping privatization of education in Canada. The impact of this initiative is, by itself, bound to be significant. However, as will be considered below, these effects are likely to interact with any GATS commitments the federal government makes in education services. And since, unlike international human rights obligations, GATS commitments are binding and can be effectively enforced, such coverage could restrict the education policies of all future Ontario governments.

Chapter 2
Coverage of public education in the GATS

2.1 The GATS covers most public service systems, including education

2.1.1 The GATS is very broad
The GATS is a very broad treaty. It covers all types of actions taken by governments that "affect" trade in services. Any government measure—whether a "law, regulation, rule, procedure, decision, administrative action, or any other form"[1]—that affects services is subject to GATS scrutiny and potential challenge. The treaty applies to actions taken by all levels of governments: federal, First Nation, provincial, state, regional, and local[2], including actions taken by school boards.

The GATS covers all the various ways in which services are supplied. The GATS defines these "modes of delivery" to be comprehensive; they include cross-border Internet or distance education, study abroad, the establishment of private schools in another country, or teaching abroad.[3] Indeed, similar treatment of similar services, no matter how the services are delivered—so-called "modal neutrality"— is a fundamental underpinning of the agreement.[4]

In principle, the GATS covers all service sectors, including education at all levels. As described later in this chapter, the GATS covers the service of classroom teaching, but also covers counselling, tutoring, administration services, sports and other extracurricular activities, cleaning, school bus transportation, and all of the myriad services that together comprise what most people understand to be our existing education system.

Finally, the GATS extends into areas that have long been considered matters purely of legitimate domestic regulation and have never before been subject to international "trade" treaties.[5] As the WTO Secretariat states, the treaty "encompasses not only measures designed to regulate trade in services directly, but also any other measures that might be designed to regulate other matters but which incidentally affect the supply of a service."[6] Indeed, the treaty applies to measures taken by members "affecting trade in services,"[7] a phrase which has recently been interpreted broadly.[8] As a result, *government measures that could modify the conditions of competition relating to education and other services—whether directly or indirectly, purposefully or unintentionally, even incidentally—could be subject to GATS scrutiny.*[9]

While the notion is likely to come as a surprise to many educators and citizens, *government measures pertaining to education at all levels in Canada are now exposed to certain of the many GATS rules and, as a result, to scrutiny and potential challenge by other GATS signatories and to oversight at the World Trade Organization.*

2.1.2 The GATS "governmental authority" exclusion is unlikely to provide substantive protection for education

When the GATS was adopted in 1994, few people recognized its importance; even fewer recognized its exceptional breadth. The application of the treaty to public service systems became subject to closer scrutiny and analysis after the publication, in 2001, of two discussion papers on the topic.[10] In order to understand the extent of the treaty, it is necessary to understand what types of services are exempted or excluded from its broad scope.

It appears to be a common belief among government representatives that the GATS does not apply to public service systems—in other words, that public services are excluded from the treaty.[11] However, the GATS contains few general exceptions or exemptions,[12] and it contains no broad exclusion for public service systems or their regulation. As the British Columbia Government discussion paper points out:[13]

> "Except for Article I:3 [considered below], the agreement contains no exclusion for public services, for public service delivery, or to protect government regulatory authority associated with public service systems. It also treats public and private service providers and delivery as "like." Similarly, the GATS treats private non-profit and private for-profit service providers and delivery identically."

The GATS does contain language in its preamble to protect "the right of Members to regulate...to meet national policy objectives,"[14] but this general provision has little legal effect, particularly when contrasted with the specific, binding obligations that are contained in the body of the treaty itself.[15]

From the standpoint of Canada's existing education system, the most relevant and promising potential protection in the GATS is provided by the so-called "governmental authority" exclusion.

Article I:3 of the agreement states:

"For the purposes of this Agreement...

(b) 'services' includes any service in any sector except services supplied in the exercise of governmental authority;

(c) 'a service supplied in the exercise of governmental authority' means any service which is supplied neither *on a commercial basis,* nor *in competi-*

tion with one or more service suppliers." (emphases added)

This exclusion is much narrower than it may appear. It is unlikely to protect Canadian education systems from GATS provisions for a number of reasons.

Firstly, in order for a service to be excluded, both criteria must apply. That is, a service must be supplied on a non-commercial basis and its delivery must not be in competition with another service supplier. The vast majority of education services in Canada are unlikely to be found to satisfy both criteria of being supplied both a) on an strictly non-commercial basis and b) by an absolute monopoly. Hence, the vast majority of Canadian education services appear to fall outside the protective Article I:3 exclusion.

Secondly, the precise scope of the critical "governmental authority" exclusion, while narrow, remains unclear. General concerns about the exclusion's lack of clarity have been raised repeatedly at the WTO in a variety of contexts.[16] It has also been noted that the exclusion's two necessary criteria are not defined in the treaty. The European Community[17], the Chairperson of the Working Party on GATS Rules,[18] and the WTO Secretariat[19] have independently observed that the meaning of one or both of the criteria is unclear.

The lack of clarity of the GATS "governmental authority" exclusion apparently has not been closely examined within the WTO. However, in its background paper on education services,[20] the WTO Secretariat appears to concede the possibility that even "basic education" may not be protected by the exclusion. The Secretariat states that:

"Basic education provided by the government *may* be considered to fall within the domain of, in the terminology of the GATS, services supplied in the exercise of governmental authority (supplied neither on a commercial basis nor in competition)." (emphasis added)

This statement, while oblique, does not deny the possibility that basic education may not, in fact, fall within the "governmental authority" exclusion.

Thirdly, while the exclusion's criteria are not defined in the GATS text, the ordinary meaning of the terms point to a very narrow exclusion. As the British Columbia discussion paper notes in its consideration of these definitions,[21] most public service systems consist of a complex mixture of public and private service delivery and suppliers that may be seen to compete against each other. The public components of these systems also frequently include some commercial aspects. Thus, using the ordinary definitions of the terms, these services would appear to be "in competition with" other service suppliers or to have "commercial" aspects—either of which would entail the service in question falling outside the protective Article I:3 exclusion and so fully subject to applicable GATS rules.

Fourthly, an examination of WTO documents supports the view that the exclusion is likely to be interpreted narrowly. In the WTO Secretariat's background paper on health and social services, the Secretariat observes that the exclusion may apply in the health sector only in exceptional circumstances: for example, where services are provided "directly through the government, free of charge."[22] More significantly, in specific reference to the sensitive areas of health and social services, the WTO Council for Trade in Services is on record asserting the "need" for the exclusion to be interpreted narrowly:

"Members drew attention to the variety of policy objectives governing the provision of health and social services, including basic welfare and equity considerations. Such considerations had led to a very substantial degree of government involvement, both as a direct provider of such services and as a regulator. However, this did not mean that the whole sector was outside the remit of the GATS; *the exceptions provided in Article I:3 of the Agreement needed to be interpreted narrowly*" (emphasis added).[23]

Fifthly, European jurisprudence involving a "similar" exclusion contained in the EC treaty strongly suggests that the GATS exclusion is likely to be interpreted very narrowly. Article 55 of the EC treaty contains an exclusion, for "activities...connected...with the exercise of official authority." The European Communities, which reportedly proposed the GATS "governmental authority" exclusion during the Uruguay round of WTO negotiations,[24] have formally indicated that they consider the GATS exclusion to be "similar" to its European model.[25] It is of particular note that the EC has also informed the WTO that the European exclusion has, without exception, been interpreted narrowly. As the EC put it:

"[t]here are no examples in the European Court of Justice jurisprudence where the Court found that an activity would fall under the scope of Article 55 [the European exclusion]" (emphasis added).[26]

Taken together, these elements indicate that *the GATS "governmental authority" exclusion is very narrow and, in the event of a dispute involving Canada's education system, is almost certain to be interpreted restrictively by a WTO dispute* tribunal. *In fact, the exclusion is so narrow that it is difficult to conceive of what, if any, protection it would afford to Canadian governments' provision, funding and regulation of public education systems.*[27]

2.2 What are education services?

2.2.1 What are services? How are they classified?

Services have been described simply as "anything that you cannot drop on your foot."[28] More broadly, services are products of human activity aimed to satisfy a human need, which do not constitute tangible commodities.[29] Services —and government regulatory measures affecting services— touch on most aspects of our everyday lives, from birth to death. As Sinclair (2000, p.22) has noted:

> "Services are much more than flipping hamburgers and waiting on tables. Heart surgery is a service. So are water purification, food distribution, and electricity transmission. Services are associated with everything we need and everything we elect governments to do."

As will be considered below, the education sector is comprised of a wide variety of services—ranging from the delivery of classroom teaching and library services to counselling services, tutoring, testing, financial management, groundskeeping, certification, speech therapy, and records keeping. All these services, and more, together make up our education systems. But not all these varied services related to education are necessarily considered, for GATS purposes, as "educational services." As we shall see, how services are classified is a key issue in assessing potential GATS impacts on education systems.

Services are now routinely classified around the world according to the provisional Central Product Classification (CPC), a general purpose classification system for goods and services that was published by the United Nations in 1991. Unlike previous classification systems, the CPC contains descriptions of services and is designed to be comprehensive, covering "the whole spectrum of outputs of heterogeneous service industries."[30] It is intended to provide a framework for international comparisons and to be used for trade, price, balance-of-payments, and various other types of statistics.

The CPC was used as a source in the preparation of the GATS.[31] The CPC was also the basis for a simpler classification list, known by the shortened version of its GATS reference number, the W/120.[32] The W/120 was used in turn by the vast majority of WTO members as the basis for their GATS commitments. While the CPC has since been revised, in part to incorporate more detailed descriptions and categories under Business Services, the W/120 (and especially the provisional CPC) is likely to remain the chief classification references during the current round of GATS re-negotiation. It must be noted, however, that the GATS Committee on Specific Commitments has adopted a pragmatic approach to classification issues. Thus, specific proposals from members could result in the adoption of modified or even ad hoc classification systems to specify members' legally binding commitments.

2.2.2 How are most education services classified in the GATS?

In order to understand the implications of GATS rules on education, it is necessary to examine how services in the education sector are classified. The classification of certain education services does not in itself entail GATS coverage. However, how services are classified is a critical aspect of determining which GATS rules now apply to particular services and which services are likely to be most at risk in future GATS re-negotiations.

Under the UN's hierarchical classification system, education services comprise Division 92 and are classified as one of the nine categories contained in "Community, Social and Personal Services" (Section 9). Education Services are then sub-divided into the following categories:

921   Primary education services
922   Secondary education services
923   Higher education services
924   Adult education services
929   Other education services.

Under the CPC, each of these categories is, in turn, divided into sub-categories.[33] These CPC categories, together with their descriptions and conditions, are reproduced in their entirety in the accompanying sidebar.[34]

A number of problems with the CPC classification system have been noted during GATS negotiations. New Zealand has proposed reviewing the classification of education services, but largely with the view to facilitating more GATS commitments in education.

2.2.3 How are other education services, or other services associated with education, classified in the GATS?

Any comprehensive system designed to arrange services in groups, according to their common characteristics, is subject to the potential for overlapping categories. This is especially true for such complex sectors as education services. It is not surprising, therefore, that services that may be closely associated with education fall outside the CPC education services category highlighted above. Child care services, for example, which are described as "pro-

International classification of "education services"

921 Primary education services

    9211   92110   Preschool education services
Pre-primary school education services. Such education services are usually provided by nursery schools, kindergartens, or special sections attached to primary schools, and aim primarily to introduce very young children to anticipated school-type environment.

            Child day-care services are classified in subclass 93321.

    9219   92190 Other primary education services
Other primary school education services as the first level. Such education services are intended to give the students a basic education in diverse subjects, and are characterized by a relatively low specialization level.

            Services related to the provision of literacy programmes for adults are classified in subclass 92400 (Adult education services n.e.c.).

922 Secondary education services

    9221   92210 General secondary education services
General school education services at the second level, first stage. Such education services consist of education that continues the basic programmes taught at the primary education level, but usually on a more subject-oriented pattern and with some beginning specialization.

    9222   92220 Higher secondary education services
General school education services at the second level, second stage. Such education services consist of general education programmes covering a wide variety of subjects involving more specialization than at the first stage. The programmes intend

to qualify students either for technical or vocational education or for university entrance without any special subject prerequisite.

9223   92230 Technical and vocational secondary education services
Technical and vocational education services below the university level. Such education services consist of programmes emphasizing subject-matter specialization and instruction in both theoretical and practical skills. They usually apply to specific professions.

9224   92240 Technical and vocational secondary school-type
education services for handicapped students
Technical and vocational secondary school-type education services specially designed to meet the possibilities and needs of handicapped students below the university level.

923   Higher education services

9231   92310 Post-secondary technical and vocational education services
Post-secondary, sub-degree technical and vocational education services. Such education services consist of a great variety of subject-matter programmes. They emphasize teaching of practical skills, but also involve substantial theoretical background instruction.

9239   92390 Other higher education services
Education services leading to a university degree or equivalent. Such education services are provided by universities or specialized professional schools. The programmes not only emphasize theoretical instruction, but also research training aiming to prepare students for participation in original work.

924   Adult education services n.e.c.

9240   92400 Adult education services not elsewhere classified

Education services for adults who are not in the regular school and university system. Such education services may be provided in day or evening classes by schools or by special institutions for adult education. Included are education services through radio or television broadcasting or by correspondence. The programmes may cover both general and vocational subjects. Services related to literacy programmes for adults are also included.

Higher education services provided within the regular education system are classified in subclass 92310 (Post-secondary technical and vocational education services) or 92390 (Other higher education services).

929   Other education services
    9290   92900 Other education services
    Education services at the first and second levels in specific subject-matters not elsewhere classified, and all other education services that are not definable by level.

Education services primarily concerned with recreational matters are classified in class 9641 (Sporting services).

Education services provided by governesses or tutors employed by private households are classified in subclass 98000 (Private households with employed persons).

Source: Source: Provisional Central Product Classification (CPC), 1991, New York, United Nations, p. vi. (ST/ESA/STAT/SER.M/77, available online at http://esa.un.org/unsd/cr/registry/regrt.asp)

viding day-time shelter and elementary, playlike teaching to small children...in nursery schools," are classified in "Social services without accommodation" (category 9332).

Similarly, even the "catch-all" category "Other education services" (929) does not include "[e]ducation services primarily concerned with recreational matters;" these are classified as "Sporting services" (9641).[35] "Other education services" also excludes "[e]ducation services provided by...tutors employed by private households," which are classified in category 98000 ("private households with employed persons"). That these services are not classified as education services is unremarkable—a seemingly inevitable consequence of attempting to "pigeonhole" diverse services.

It is more significant that some services that are widely seen to be fundamental aspects of education systems are also excluded from the CPC education services category. For example, library services—including those provided to students—are classed not as an education service, but as a cultural service:

"96 Recreational, Cultural and Sporting Services
963 Library, archive, museum and other cultural services
9631 Library and archive services
96311 Library services
  Services of libraries of all kinds. Documentation services, i.e. collection, cataloguing, whether manually or computer-aided, and retrieval services of documents. The services may be provided to the general public or to a special clientele, such as students, scientists, employers, members, etc."

In fact, a more detailed examination shows that the CPC category of education services is rather more narrow than it initially appears. For example, the descriptions of education services contained in the CPC repeatedly refer to "programmes," and to "subjects" and "instruction." This suggests that the category is designed primarily to include classroom teaching and similar types of instruction, rather than the rich variety of related services that make up what most citizens consider the education system. In other words, not all of the many services that make up Canada's existing education system are contained within the CPC education services category; these services are widely dispersed throughout the CPC classification system.

What kinds of services fall outside the education services category?

Services that fall outside the education services category include many key aspects of our education system: special services involving students, services involved with maintaining infrastructure, and the administration and management of education services and facilities. The examples of coaching (sporting services) and tutoring (private households with employed persons) have already been noted. There are many other examples; these include student testing, secretarial services, and teacher recruitment, and also extend to school administration, pension fund administration, and labour union services (*see sidebar*).[36]

This list highlights a number of important aspects of the classification scheme underlying the GATS. The list of educational services that are not included under the heading "education services" is extensive. It also contains many categories that may overlap with those in the education services categories. Moreover, as is the case

Education related services that fall outside the "education services" category

Testing students' academic achievement
 (Other business services not elsewhere classified (n.e.c.), CPC 87909)
Providing guidance and counselling services to students or parents
 (Guidance and counselling services n.e.c. related to children, CPC 93322)
Providing meals or snacks to students
 (Food serving services, CPC 642)
Providing district and school secretarial services
 (Other business services n.e.c., CPC 87909)
Cleaning school and other buildings
 (Building cleaning services, CPC 874)
Providing school bus transportation
 (Interurban special transportation, CPC 71214)
Maintaining student records
 (Data processing services, CPC 843; Other computer services, CPC 849)
Managing, operating, inspecting and administering schools
 (Administrative educational services, CPC 91121; Management consulting services, CPC 865)
Recruiting teachers, administrators and other staff
 (Placement and supply services of personnel, CPC 872)
Maintaining good community relations
 (Public relations services, CPC 86506)
Pension fund administration
 (Government employee pension schemes, CPC 9132)
Labour union services
 (Services furnished by trade unions, CPC 95200)
School support services provided by parent committees
 (Services furnished by other membership organizations n.e.c., CPC 9599)

Source: Provisional Central Product Classification (CPC), 1991, New York, United Nations, p. vi. (ST/ESA/STAT/SER.M/77, available online at http://esa.un.org/unsd/cr/registry/regrt.asp)

throughout the CPC, there are no distinctions made within the categories for public—as opposed to private—service delivery. Nor are there distinctions made in private education services between non-profit and for-profit service delivery or service providers. While these distinctions are often critical from a public policy perspective, as we shall see, they simply do not exist in the GATS taxonomy, where a service is simply a service.

Finally, the services in this list and throughout the CPC include all modes of services delivery. Hence, a math course provided over the Internet may be deemed to be "like" a math course provided through a correspondence course, which in turn may be "like" a math course provided in a classroom.

In short, *every education-related activity of any kind, in any form, delivered by any individual or organization, is in principle classified under the UN service classification scheme. Moreover, how a specific service is classified in this scheme is critical in determining which GATS rules and obligations apply.*

2.3 Which GATS rules now apply to education?

The next step in determining which GATS obligations apply to which education services is to examine the scope of application of the two main types of GATS rules—namely, general rules and specific commitments.

2.3.1 GATS general rules already apply "across the board"

The GATS contains certain general rules that apply to all services and all service sectors—even those where a member has not made a specific commitment. The two general provisions that are most relevant to the education sector, namely most-favoured-nation treatment and transparency, are considered in turn below, while the GATS rules on Domestic Regulation are considered later.

The GATS Most-Favoured-Nation (MFN) treatment

The GATS MFN obligation (Article II) is one of the treaty's general rules that apply unconditionally and automatically to all services, including education-related services. MFN requires that the best treatment accorded to any foreign service provider must be accorded "immediately and unconditionally" to all foreign service providers.

In general terms, this powerful provision has the practical effect of consolidating any commercialization, privatization, or other market-opening measures involving foreign service providers. It may also greatly increase the constituency for commercialization and privatization, and for resisting future efforts to reverse such initiatives.[37]

The GATS Transparency rules

GATS transparency rules require members to publish all existing measures, at all levels of government, that "pertain to or affect the operation" of the treaty. Article III also requires Members to inform the WTO Council for Trade in Services of any new measure, or changes to existing, measures that "significantly affect trade in services" covered by that member's specific commitments. Members are also required to establish enquiry points to provide information to other members on any changes or new measures affecting services.

While these GATS transparency rules may not appear to be particularly onerous, they introduce new administrative demands on governments that may be particularly onerous for school boards and local, state, or provincial governments that administer education systems. More significantly, several GATS proponents have indicated that GATS transparency rules are a precondition or necessary tool for further liberalization in subsequent rounds of negotiations.[38]

2.3.2 GATS specific rules, which apply only to listed services

In addition to these general rules, the GATS also contains conditional obligations. These powerful provisions, which include National Treatment and Market Access, apply only to those sectors where a member has undertaken specific commitments.

The GATS National Treatment rule

The GATS national treatment rule (Article XVII) requires members to extend the best treatment that is given domestically to other GATS members. Broader than generally recognized, this non-discrimination provision requires that every advantage given to a domestic service or service provider must be accorded to a like foreign service or service provider. Indeed, GATS Article XVII:2 and 3 stipulate that national treatment of foreign services and providers extends beyond treatment that is "formally identical" to that accorded domestically; members must accord foreign services and providers "no less favourable... conditions of competition." Significantly, this doctrine— treatment to ensure effective equality of conditions of competition—has recently been applied to the MFN article.[39]

Together with the expansive scope of the GATS, this rigorous standard for non-discrimination ensures that dispute settlement panels will find many government measures, which on their surface are origin- and nationality-neutral, GATS-inconsistent. As Sinclair[40] notes, "It need only be argued that such measures are capable of altering the conditions of competition either in favour of domestic services and service providers (national treatment) or in favour of certain, but not all, foreign services and services providers (most-favoured-nation)."

The GATS Market Access rule

Like the national treatment obligation, the GATS rules on market access (Article XVI) are onerous provisions that apply only to those services that a government lists in its schedule of specific commitments. This article (subsection 2(a)-(c)) states that in sectors where market access commitments are made, members "shall not maintain or adopt ...limitations on...the number of service suppliers[,]...the total value of service transactions[,]...or the total number of service operations." It must be emphasized that, in principle, these market access prohibitions are absolute, preventing outright such numerical limits on services or service suppliers, even if they do not discriminate against foreign services or suppliers.

It must be re-emphasized that these conditional obligations apply only to services that have been listed by GATS signatories in their schedule of commitments, and then only to the extent specified by the signatory. Canada as yet has made no specific commitments in the education services sectors as delineated in the CPC classification system. Canada has, however, made specific commitments in the following related sub-sectors:[41]

> Other Business Services, Management consulting services (CPC 865)
>> General management consulting services (86501)
>> Human resources management consulting services (86504)

Building-cleaning services (874)
Other business services (879)
Construction work for buildings, including commercial buildings (512)
Food retailing services (631)

Though the impact of these commitments are naturally likely to be less direct than other impacts of the treaty, they cannot be ignored. Selected impacts of such commitments are touched on in Chapters 3 and 4.

2.3.3 Other GATS provisions

The built-in GATS commitment to repeated re-negotiation

All WTO member governments have consented to the overarching commitment, contained in Article XIX, to broaden and deepen the agreement through successive rounds of future negotiations. The intent is to achieve "a progressively higher level of liberalization," largely by "increasing the general level of specific commitments undertaken by Members" and through new rules on domestic regulation. Given the prospect of repeated GATS re-negotiation, any protection afforded to education-related services, for example, cannot be considered permanent and may indeed have the perverse effect of drawing increased attention to these excluded services and so making them even more vulnerable in future negotiating rounds.[42]

The GATS Domestic Regulation rules

In GATS Article VI:4, members agreed that the WTO Council for Trade in Services, "through appropriate bodies it may establish," shall "develop any necessary disciplines" to ensure that "measures relating to qualification requirements ...[and] technical standards and licensing requirements do not constitute unnecessary barriers to trade in services." Negotiations are now under way to carry out this mandate. It is important to understand that these new restrictions are specifically and exclusively intended to constrain non-discriminatory regulatory measures taken by governments.

The effect of the domestic regulation provisions could be to introduce into the revised GATS a new and more restrictive test—a finer screen—through which government measures are required to pass. As a result, even government measures that are fully consistent with the arduous non-discrimination rules contained in the GATS MFN and national treatment articles, and even those that are consistent with the GATS market access provisions, could be found to violate the GATS under the proposed domestic regulation restrictions.

Moreover, while no agreement has been reached, these so-called "disciplines" could apply across-the-board to all service sectors, including education and not be limited to service sectors for which member governments have listed specific commitments in their national schedules. Under these proposed rules, governments would be obliged to demonstrate that non-discriminatory regulations were "necessary" to achieve a legitimate objective, and that no alternative measure was available that was less commercially restrictive.[43]

There are no public indications that any WTO member is opposed to developing these "disciplines" under Article VI:4. However, these provisions are likely to attract increased attention from GATS critics. For example, the Canadian Environmental Law Association's Michelle Swenarchuk has called the exercise "a wholly unwarranted intrusion of trade law into important domestic public safety laws".[44] These negotiations are also likely to become contentious even among some proponents as governments at all levels come to understand just how far-reaching are the proposals under consideration.

Chapter 3
The impact of the current GATS treaty amid the increasing commercialization of education

It would be easy to underestimate the impact of the GATS on Canada's public education system.

At first glance, the GATS does not appear to pose serious or immediate threats to public education. Canada and most other countries have not yet agreed to apply the treaty's toughest rules to the sector. Public education is acknowledged to be politically sensitive, and is not one of the sectors specifically targeted in the current round of GATS re-negotiations. And, in the short term, the immediate effects of commercialization and privatization, which have been taking place outside the ambit of treaty negotiations, seem far more serious than the pressures arising from the services treaty itself.

It would be wrong to conclude, however, that WTO rules do not affect public education. The treaty already casts a long shadow over it. The effects of the current treaty, already significant in themselves, can be expected to become more important in the future. If ignored by citizens and public educators, the future effects of the GATS, including consolidating and reinforcing commercialization trends and circumscribing governments' regulatory ability in the education field, could prove to be both profound and unprecedented. Indeed, the GATS is a 'work-in-progress'—an unfinished framework agreement designed for continuous expansion through perpetual re-negotiation. While not likely to result in immediate, sweeping changes, it could entail an inexorable ratcheting-down of public policy options.

Finally, as will be discussed below, the threats to some aspects of education could be immediate. Internal government documents recently obtained under Access to Information provide evidence that Canada is poised to make GATS commitments in private education services in the current round of GATS re-negotiations—a move that could expose important aspects of Canada's public education system to GATS challenges.

Before considering the various ways in which the GATS threatens public education, it is important to examine the context of continuous commercialization and privatization in which GATS negotiations are taking place.

3.1 The context for GATS negotiations: increasing commercialization and privatization of education

For many Canadians and citizens around the world, applying so-called free-market principles to public education seems an incongruous notion at best. How could the application of market forces address the perennial problem of inequality within our public education systems? Wouldn't allocation of resources according to ability to pay lead to even greater inequality? Wouldn't the introduction of the profit motive into public education make it more expensive for most citizens? And what is public education if not a system that, for some important, well-established societal reasons, is largely shielded from the cutthroat world of for-profit business?

However foreign the concept may strike Canadians, the application of market forces to education is becoming increasingly common. Local schools increasingly look to private funding to supplement their strapped budgets.

Commercial education service providers promise solutions to teachers' and administrators' needs, and offer access to equipment and educational materials that public schools increasingly cannot otherwise afford. And some provincial governments allocate public funding directly to private schooling. These changes have often accompanied by reforms to our public education systems. In the United States, the commercialization and privatization of public education is further under way.

As will be examined in the subsequent sections, the commercial pressures that already exist, while they are independent of the treaty, reinforce the effects of the GATS and, in turn, are reinforced by it. However, before considering these interactions and the various ways in which the GATS threatens public education, it is important to review the numerous aspects of commercialization that already exist in the public education system.

3.1.1 Public schools generate commercial revenue

Canadians annually spend almost $2.3 billion—equal to $400 per student—in private payments for elementary and secondary level education.[1] This represents the amount, over and above our tax contributions, which Canadians directly pay through various fees and charges for all forms of schooling, including private schools.

Nationally, private contributions amount to 6% of total spending on elementary and secondary education. As the table shows, private payments for schooling vary widely across the country. They are currently highest in Manitoba and British Columbia, where they account for 9% of total spending (almost $600 per student), and lowest in Prince Edward Island and in New Brunswick, where they account for 1% of total spending (about $50 per student). Private payments in Ontario are 5% of total spending and somewhat under $400 per student.

The available data do not identify how much private revenue is generated by public schools, as opposed to private schools. It should be noted also that these figures are based on administrative data collected by provincial ministries of education, which may not include occasional informal fees and fundraising at public schools.

The following are some common ways in which public schools generate revenue from private sources. Some forms, like incidental fees and fundraising for field trips and other activities, are not new. Others, like recruiting international fee-paying students, are novel. As well as raising concerns about equity, the increasing reliance of public schools on these various sources of private funding introduces elements of commerce and competition into the operation of public school systems.

Parental fees and fundraising

Incidental fees and school fundraising are a well-established source of supplementary funding for most public schools. While these sources have traditionally been used to pay for field trips and other special activities, there is evidence that out-of-pocket payments are increasingly being used to fund essential classroom materials and activities. In most cases, the fees are waived for children whose families are unable to pay. Nevertheless, they are a source of inequity between schools, as schools in relatively wealthy neighbourhoods are able to plan more supplementary activities than those in poorer neighbourhoods which are unable to raise the same level of funds.

A survey of Ontario schools found an increase in fundraising activity by all schools. The average amount raised was $7,000 in 2000/2001, compared to $5,000 in

1998/99. The prevalence of fundraising for essential supplies was a particular concern. Schools reported that 27% of the total amount raised was directed to textbooks, computers, and classroom supplies. Over 60% of schools raised funds for library books; half raised funds for classroom supplies, computers, and software; and a quarter raised funds for textbooks.[2]

This growing reliance on fundraising is coupled with large disparities in the fundraising capacities of different schools. The top 10% of fundraising schools, which are located in high income communities, raised an average of $1,400 per class, compared to $160 per class in the bottom 10% of fundraising schools. Put another way, the group of 78 schools that raised over $20,000 each generated as much money as the group of 508 schools that raised under $10,000 each.[3]

These disparities are raising concerns about growing inequities between public schools. As one participant in the study commented:

"We have an active school council that raises a fair amount of money. This is a good thing. However, all of us on council are concerned at the changes in the direction that our money goes. Now we are directing much of it to what we consider essential services like classroom supplies and textbooks. We are particularly concerned over the potential for two-tiered public schooling. We are able to maintain essential services for our children. What about those schools that do not have strong school councils?"[4]

There is a longer history of these issues in the United States, where fundraising in some school districts reaches into the hundreds of thousands of dollars. Parents in Public School 321 in Brooklyn, for instance, raised US$100,000 in 1997 to pay the salaries of an art and music teacher.[5] At a fundraising auction in a wealthy part of Houston, one parent paid $20,000 for a reserved parking space in front of the school.

These activities have raised dilemmas for school authorities when parents seek to ensure that the funds they raise benefit their own children. According to analyst Andrew Stark, school authorities in the U.S. have tried to ensure that private funding of this sort does not create inequities *within* a particular school, but they have not addressed the inequities created *between* schools:

"From superintendents to school boards, and from principles to parents, intraschool equity is the abiding norm across America, the mother principle to which parental fundraising must recur. But it is useless as a standard for drawing distinctions between more or less egregious kinds of interschool equity."[6]

Stark advocates a model pioneered in Portland, Oregon, that permits parents to raise funds for extra teachers for their children, but requires them to donate one-third of the money they raise to a district-wide fund, to which schools in high poverty areas can apply for grants. While this compromise may help to redress inequities between schools, it illustrates how private fundraising has become institutionalized in many parts of the U.S., and how even efforts to redistribute funds more equitably can introduce new forms of competition between public schools.

Sponsorships
Sponsorships are another well-established source of private funding that has lately taken on novel forms. It's

not new for a local business to pay for the scoreboard in a school arena, or the uniforms for school sports teams. But when large corporations offer equipment, events, and cash in return for marketing opportunities, it raises new questions about the commercialization of our schools.

In some cases, the sponsor receives goodwill in return for its contribution. For instance, the Wal-Mart chain, which has drawn resentment in many communities for undercutting local merchants, has "adopted" seven schools in Nova Scotia. As well as providing free computers and discounts on school supplies and equipment, Wal-Mart funds occasional extracurricular activities. These activities would not otherwise be possible, according to the principal of one of the sponsored schools (see sidebar).[7]

In other cases, corporate advertising provides a more tangible return to the sponsor:
- Some textbooks in the Bluewater District School Board in Ontario now sport a TD bank logo.
- The Surrey, B.C. school board permits advertising on school buses, raising $10,000 for a Pepsi ad.
- The Delta, B.C. school board recently approved a policy to allow similar advertising in and around its schools.[8]

In these cases, the schools engage in a clearly commercial service: placing advertisements for commercial sponsors. In this respect, public schools compete with other providers of advertising locations, and possibly other public institutions. To the degree that these kinds of arrangements become an accepted part of school finances, they undermine the "public" character of Canadian education and could have important GATS implications.

Wal-Mart "adopts" schools

The Halifax Daily News
Monday, January 8, 2001
(excerpt)

Wal-Mart school adoptees profiting
By Peter McLaughlin

A one-of-a-kind relationship between U.S. retail giant Wal-Mart and seven Nova Scotia schools "adopted" by the company a year ago appears to be paying off for both students and schools. Individual students have snagged
gifts and store-sponsored outings.

The schools received free computers and store discounts.

"The only way I can describe it is fantastic," says Kevin Deveaux, principal of Lakevale School in Sydney, a Primary to Grade 4 school with just 60 students that sits almost at the edge of the local Wal-Mart parking lot.

Sydney's Mayflower Mall Wal-Mart has also donated sports equipment such as balls and hula-hoops, a computer, and taken students to McDonald's and the theatre at Christmas.

The store also gives the school special deals on school supplies and equipment.

"We have a lot of low-income families, and, without Wal-Mart supporting us, the money we're using for a lot of extracurricular activities at no cost to children would not be possible," Deveaux says.

International recruitment

Globalization has greatly increased the potential for cash-strapped public schools to recruit fee-paying international students. Such recruitment has indeed become a component of Canadian trade policy. In February, 2002, representatives from Nanaimo, B.C.'s School District No. 68 joined the prime minister, federal and provincial trade officials, and other participants in the latest "Team Canada" trade promotion trip to Germany and Russia.

The district's international education program offers foreign students English immersion, together with the full range of Grade 9-12 curriculum. It charges international students $11,000 per year and not only pays for itself, but also contributes revenue to the school district. A district representatives was recently reported to have enthused: "We'll take as many new international students as we can get."[9]

Dozens of Canadian school boards now actively recruit international students through services provided by the Canadian Education Centre Network, a wholly-owned subsidiary of the Vancouver-based Asia Pacific Foundation of Canada. For a fee, the CEC will feature these schools in its promotional material, in its circuit of "education fairs", and in the 20 offices it maintains around the world.

CEC promotional material includes the "Study in Canada!" web site, which attracts millions of prospective students annually. It has the appearance of an official Government of Canada web site, but is owned by CEC Networks. Twenty-seven public school boards and six individual public schools are promoted on the site, along with private schools and post-secondary institutions.

The Vancouver School Board offers schooling to international students for an annual fee of $11,000, or $1,100 per month, for short-term study, plus a home-stay placement of $730 to $750 per month. The Ottawa-Carleton District School Board is slightly less expensive, at $10,000 annually and $700 per month for home-stay. Saskatoon Catholic Schools are a better bargain: $8,500 per month, with a home-stay fee of $500 per month.[10]

As well as competing with one another to attract students, public schools compete with private schools, which are also promoted by CEC Networks and advertised on

Canadian Education Centre Networks

CEC Networks has grown rapidly since it was founded in 1995. It has attracted over 270 institutional clients, including school boards, private schools, universities, community colleges and training associations.

Annual membership fees are $6,000 for public and private schools and boards with over 1,500 students ($3,000 for those with under 1,500 students). In return for this fee, the CEC helps to recruit international students through its international offices, its education fairs, and its promotional material.

There are 20 CEC offices around the world, mainly in large Asian and Latin American centres. Staff at these offices distribute promotional material, and test, interview and counsel prospective students on behalf of CEC clients. Several of these offices enjoy a close association with Canadian government missions. The CEC Vietnam office, for instance, is located next door to the Consulate General of Canada in Ho Chi Minh City. The CEC Argentina office shares space with the Canadian Tourism Commission.

For additional fees ranging between $1,000 and $3,000, depending on the market, school boards can be represented at "education fairs" which CEC organizes around the world. In 1998/99, 1,052 educational institutions participated in the 31 education fairs held in Seoul, Hong Kong, Taipai, Buenos Aires, Mexico City, Sao Paolo, and other large centres throughout Asia, Latin America, and in some European and Middle East countries.

CEC Networks receives substantial federal government contributions, in addition to fees from public educational institutions. In 1998/99, its total revenue was $7.2 million, of which $2.6 million was contributed by the Canadian International Development Agency and $380,000 was contributed by the Department of Foreign Affairs and International Trade. (CEC remitted $479,000 to CIDA from program revenues earned in the same year.)

Sources: CEC Network 1998/99 Annual Report; CEC web site (www.cecnetwork.org); and Study in Canada! web site (www.studyincanada.com).

its Study in Canada! web site. Forty-four private schools are promoted in this way. Like the public schools, the private schools tout the high quality of the education they offer and the safety of their communities as principal attractions for prospective students.

Among the private schools competing with the Vancouver School Board are Malaspina International High School, located in Nanaimo, B.C., which charges $12,000 tuition, and St. John's International High School in Vancouver, which charges $11,000 tuition (plus over $1,000 in mandatory supplementary fees).[11] Public and private schools are clearly competing for the same pool of potential students. They recruit through the same agency; they offer equivalent services; and they charge comparable fees.

Most international students come from Asia, particularly South Korea, Hong Kong, and Taiwan. In 1997, the CEC office in Seoul fielded more than 25,000 inquiries from students of all ages, of which over 8,000 received a visa to study in Canada. Numbers dropped off the following year, however, in the wake of the Asian financial crisis. The CEC has since increased its recruitment efforts in other markets, particularly in Latin America where the number of international recruitments has grown dramatically. The CEC office in Mexico City fielded over 12,000 inquiries in 1998, with more than 2,500 applicants receiving immigration papers.[12]

The majority of students recruited by the CEC are destined for post-secondary institutions. CEC staff estimate, however, that large school boards in British Columbia, which is the most popular destination, host as many as 500 to 600 foreign fee-paying students at any one time. At over $10,000 each, this represents a significant source of revenue. Enrolments are also high in schools in Winnipeg, Manitoba, and Alberta, due to well-established recruitment programs in those provinces.[13]

As well as providing additional revenue, which may help offset provincial funding cuts, international students can contribute to the cultural wealth and diversity of their host schools and communities. However, as will be considered below, the active recruitment of these students by public school boards could have troublesome GATS implications where public school boards act as commercial service providers, competing with one another and with private schools to attract additional clients.

The prevalence of this recruitment activity has led New Zealand to propose adding a definition for "education agency services" to the CPC classification for education services.[14] Its proposal would make the business of organizations such as CEC Networks part of the education sector, thereby further blurring the distinction between public and commercial education and augmenting the constituency with an interest in trade liberalization within the education sector.

Public-private partnerships

Financial pressures have prompted some public school boards to seek private sector financing for new schools and other capital projects. There are various forms of public- private partnerships, in which a private corporation builds and owns a new facility with a long-term lease to a public school board. This saves the school board from borrowing investment capital, but involves ongoing operating costs and liabilities over the term of the lease, which typically outweigh any short-term advantage.

In the mid-1990s, the Nova Scotia government embarked on a massive public-private partnership project to build over 50 new schools for $350 million. The project was cancelled in June 2000 because it had proved too costly: the 38 schools constructed under the plan had cost taxpayers $32 million more than was estimated. The province reverted to financing future school construction out of public funds.[15]

Despite falling far short of their promised benefits, there is a strong industry lobby for public-private partnerships. School boards in other parts of the country are also involved in public-private partnerships. The school board in Moncton, N.B. leases a school from a Fredricton company, Greenarm Corporation, which financed construction of the school through Mutual Life Assurance Co. of Canada. In Alberta, the provincial government is backing a deal between the Catholic board in Edmonton and Sobeys West to construct a combined school and grocery store. Sobeys West would contribute $3.2 million towards construction of the proposed school—dubbed 'Shopping Cart High'—in return for being able to build an IGA store on land reserved for public uses. Though Edmonton Catholic School Board has already received provincial government approval and a commitment of $12.6 million in provincial funding, City Council has not approved rezoning for the land because the project doesn't accord with provincial law regulating the attachment of commercial use to municipal land. The future of the project remains unclear.[16]

While different from other forms of commercialization, private sector financing of public school construction is another way in which the operation of public schools resemble commercial operations. Such arrangements, similar to the proposed public-private partnership for a Vancouver water treatment facility, are often controversial[17] and raise novel and troubling issues under the GATS and other international treaties.[18]

3.1.2 Commercial services operate within public schools

Another form of commercialization involves public spending on commercial services provided within the public school system. For the growing commercial education industry, these public education budgets are much larger and more lucrative sources of potential revenue than are direct payments by families and other sources of private income. These commercial services range from busing and specialist programs, which have long been provided by outside contractors in most Canadian jurisdictions, to the burgeoning field of test preparation and private tutoring services and still-speculative on-line education ventures, such as "learning channels." As this form of commercialization proliferates, the number of companies seeking access to large public revenue streams will increase. These companies, many of which are large multinational operations, will no doubt consider the GATS a useful tool to influence government policies in their favour.

Specialists, enhanced programs, busing and other commercial services

Specialists, busing, and other commercial services have a long-standing presence in public schools. Most public school boards have contracts with private providers of a number of these services, including the following examples:
- speech therapists, psychologists and other professional specialists;
- performing artists, musicians, and entertainers who perform in schools; and
- busing.

Commercial providers of these services have in many cases replaced publicly-provided services as public staffing and funding for these services has decreased. Busing, which is typically provided by a private operator, is most relevant from a GATS perspective. It often accounts for a significant share of school board expenditures and often involves large busing operators with a strong commercial interest in retaining their access to these public budgets.

Tutoring and test-preparation services

For many years there has been a small market for private tutors providing remedial and supplementary assistance to students outside of school hours. The growth of franchise tutoring operations, such as Kumon and Sylvan Learning Systems, suggest that this market has grown, and will grow further as provinces implement new standardized tests in elementary and secondary schools. And, as the reporting of school results increases pressure to demonstrate achievement, schools are likely to integrate tutoring and test-preparation services into the regular curriculum.

This industry has grown rapidly in the U.S., where long-established test-preparation companies have developed new products directed to elementary and secondary schools.[19] One U.S. company, Educational Testing Service, which administers the SAT, GRE, LSAT, MCAT, and other tests, has recently gained a foothold in public education in Canada. ETS was awarded a contract by the Ontario government to develop a qualifying test for prospective teachers.[20] ETS is one of twelve members of the National Committee for International Trade in Education (NCITE), a self-described "collective voice on trade issues for U.S. higher education and training" that advises US Trade Representative on GATS negotiations.[21]

The issue of "testing services" is explicitly on the negotiating table in the current GATS negotiations, where it gets special mention in the Unites States' proposal on education services. In its proposal to other GATS members, the U.S. advocates that the coverage of "education services" should be "clarified" so as to explicitly include testing services. While this proposal focuses on higher education, adult education and training, it notes that "testing services generally are related to all types of education." Moreover, according to the U.S., testing services are "a fundamental and essential part of the learning process" and include "designing and administering tests, as well as evaluating test results."[22]

"Learning channels" and on-line educational packages
A number of Canadian companies are attempting to emulate U.S. companies that have found commercial opportunities in providing public schools with access to television, computer and internet technologies.

The best-known venture was Youth News Network, which offered schools free television equipment in return for viewing a daily 12-minute current-affairs show in their classrooms, which was funded partially through the sale of advertising spots. Despite strong initial interest from schools in six provinces, the YNN venture floundered after opposition from parent groups objecting to the terms of the YNN contracts and to the devotion of curriculum time to a commercial television program. Athena Educational Partners Inc., which owns YNN, has since turned to developing Internet-based services and software designed to help students and their parents keep school work and records up to date.[23]

The giant Thomson Corporation has also invested heavily in on-line educational publishing. Formerly Canada's largest newspaper chain, Thomson has divested most of its news holdings other than the *Globe and Mail*, and invested heavily in acquisitions and joint ventures to build up its Thomson Learning division. It aims to provide a comprehensive range of educational materials, from the elementary level to professional training. Products include assessment programs, test-preparation, career guidance and both traditional and electronic textbooks. In Canada, Nelson publishing, which has long been owned by Thomson Corporation, has been renamed Nelson Thomson Learning. Its products include a full range of K-12 textbooks and assessment programs.

Like other educational publishers, Thomson is attempting to make the transition from a traditional publisher to one that focuses on electronic delivery of educational material. An academic observer of the educational publishing industry describes an ambitious business agenda premised on an accelerated privatization of education at all levels:

"The list of [Thomson's acquisition and partnership] activities goes on.... [A]ll in all, this represents a major initiative, which, when viewed as a whole, represents the development of an educational institution which dwarfs even the largest university.... [T]he agenda, I think, is pretty clear—online learning materials, from kindergarten through university and beyond, become commodities, paid for on a per-student license basis, and are widely available on demand— post-secondary education becomes almost exclusively the domain of private enterprise: primary and secondary education gradually moves out of the public sphere, replaced by charter schools, home schooling, and similar enterprises (these are made possible by widely available teaching materials, available at reasonable cost from Thomson)."[24]

While this vision of wholesale privatization of schooling may seem implausible to some, Thomson Corp. has invested heavily in the expectation that demand for its commercial services will increase from public schools, individuals, and private institutions.[25]

3.1.3 Public funding of private education

Private schools currently receive public funding in the provinces of Quebec, Manitoba, Saskatchewan, Alberta, and British Columbia. As described in the accompanying sidebar, most of these provinces provide a per-pupil grant directly to the schools. Alberta recently raised its support to 60% of the basic instruction grant provided to public schools, equivalent to $2,422 per pupil. Québec, which spends more on public education, grants private schools $3,200 per pupil at the secondary level. About 15% of secondary students in Québec are enrolled in private schools.[26]

In contrast to these direct grant systems, the Ontario government tax rebate will subsidize private school tuition fees through the income tax system. By providing a tax benefit to families with children in private schools, it will indirectly benefit those private schools. Ontario will provide a tax credit of 10% of private school tuition in 2002, up to $700 per child, increasing to 50% of tuition in 2006, up to $3,500 per child.

The Ontario government touts its tax credit for private schools as a measure to 'support equity and choice in education,'[27] but the evidence available to date supports the view that it is 'a voucher system in disguise.' The government has made clear that the same subsidy will apply to all income levels; it will not be targeted to lower income earners. As with voucher systems, it supports a form of choice modelled on market competition rather than on accommodating diversity within the public system. As the system is implemented, it can be expected to not only bleed funding from public schools, but also to bring public schools more directly into competition with their private counterparts. That may well be one of the primary, unstated objectives of the Ontario government initiative.

3.1.4 Commercial public schools: The emergence of Education Management Organizations (EMOs)

In Canada, the United States is known, among other things, for its private health maintenance organizations (HMOs) and for a health system that leaves approximately 40 million U.S. citizens with no health insurance coverage. What is not well known is that the United States has recently fostered the rapid expansion of private, for-profit firms known as EMOs—short for education maintenance organizations. More properly considered *education management organizations*[28], these companies manage public schools, including charter schools, for profit. According to education analysts, EMOs are one of the fastest growing components of a burgeoning "education industry."[29]

Ever since University of Chicago economist Milton Friedman advocated a tax-financed national voucher system for public schools in 1962, conservative economists and think-tanks have proposed various models of competition and incentives for the education system.[30]

Under a system of school vouchers, every public school student would receive a "chit" or voucher covering the tuition costs at the school of the parents' choice. The theory is that parents of students in bad schools would switch their children to better schools, and that schools that failed to improve would see their funds dwindle and eventually be forced to close.[31] Critics contend that a voucher system would exacerbate inequality by creaming off the ablest students, leaving their former schools and other students in worse shape.

Free market advocates have also proposed the establishment of charter schools to generate competition between schools. In many cases, the holder of a school charter—which generally entails the supply of both school facilities and management—is permitted to be a for-profit company. In other cases, charter holders are allowed to contract part or all of the management and school operation to a for-profit company. Since the passage of the first state law allowing charter schools in 1991, the charter school movement has expanded rapidly: 37 states now allow charter schools to operate.[32]

Contract schools, another type of commercialization, have also begun to emerge. In these cases, school facilities already exist and service contracts are granted to manage and operate them. While still rare for traditional and politically sensitive K-12 instruction in the United States, the number of these contract schools has grown steadily.

The new phenomenon of education management organizations is thus broader than both vouchers and charter schools. EMOs do not depend on a voucher system for their success. Nor are EMOs restricted to charter schools, though the rapid increase of charter schools has greatly benefited these organizations. As Arizona State University education researcher Alex Molnar and colleagues[33] put it:

"Companies have always profited from selling necessary supplies to schools, but the concept of making a profit from the administration and practice of K-12 public education itself is new. The 1990s were a period of rapid expansion for what is now called the 'education industry. One of the fastest growing sections of that industry is that of [EMOs —] companies managing public schools, particularly charter schools, for profit...The charter school movement has been a boon to EMOs."

The education management industry has indeed expanded rapidly. The most recent directory of EMOs, produced by Molnar's research organization, published in December 2000 and updated in February 2001, profiles 21 companies that manage 285 schools in 22 states. These EMOs include Edison Schools (84 schools), Leona Group (34), National Heritage Academies (27), Beacon Education Management (25), Advantage Schools (15), Charter School Administrative Services (15), Mosaica Education (12), Tesseract Group (11), and White Hat Management (9).[34]

A brief examination of Edison Schools, Inc—the largest EMO operating in the U.S.—highlights the new difficulties in distinguishing clearly between public education and commercial education. The Edison example shows that education can be seen as a big business like any other. It contrasts sharply "the gap between the demands of the bottom line inherent in for-profit Education Management Organizations and their avowed desire to help American public education."[35] And, from the standpoint of the GATS, it clearly demonstrates that commercial, for-profit education service providers can operate side by side—and in direct competition—with public, non-profit providers in the very heart of what has long been considered the public education system.

Examining Edison Schools, Inc. – America's largest EMO

A prominent U.S. market guide[1] provides the following overview of the company:

"Edison Schools, Inc. is a private operator of public schools serving students from kindergarten through 12th grade, contracting with local school districts to assume educational and operational responsibility for schools in return for per-pupil funding....

The company opened its first four schools in August 1995, and has grown in every subsequent year. In the 2001-2002 school year, Edison expects to enrol approximately 75,000 students in 136 schools located in 22 states and the District of Columbia. [In addition, d]uring the summer of 2001... Edison served approximately 12,000 students in its summer school program."

Edison Schools' website[2] notes that it "takes responsibility for implementing the educational program, technology plans, and management systems, and is accountable to a local authority for the performance of the school." Each school in its network "automatically becomes part of the national system of [Edison] partnership schools, literally linked through Edison's electronic message, conferencing, and information system."

Significantly, from a GATS perspective, "Edison schools remain public schools, open to all students and funded with tax dollars."[3]

Edison is reportedly "the only major provider of contract schools for traditional K-12 instruction in the United States" and currently has few direct competitors in the private sector as other education firms "focus primarily or exclusively on operating charter schools, rather than contracting with school districts."[4]

As two *U.S. News* reporters put it:

"Most of the other publicly traded companies in the fast-growing education industry focus on corporate training or postsecondary education. Edison, by contrast, has taken aim squarely at the giant and politically sensitive market of kindergarten through 12th grade."[5]

Edison's executive officers include prominent individuals with a range of business and other experience:[6]
- Board Chairman Benno Schmidt, Jr. previously served as President of Yale University and Dean of the Columbia University School of Law.
- President and CEO Christopher Whittle previously headed Whittle Communications L.P., which developed magazines and Channel One, an advertising-supported daily news and information television program for schools.
- Chief Financial Officer James Starr was previously chief financial officer for a private health services company and senior accountant at Deloitte and Touche.
- Chief Education Officer John E. Chubb, who co-founded Edison Schools, is co-author of the 1990 book on school competition entitled "Politics, Markets and America's Schools".

Edison's board includes other individuals who have previous employment experience in education, including a former chancellor of the New York City Public Schools (Ramon Cortines), a former general superintendent of the Detroit public schools (Deborah McGriff), and a former superintendent of Rochester Public Schools (Manuel Rivera).

The board also includes individuals drawn from the publishing industry—Children's Television Workshop, Sesame Street (Joan Cooney); Scholastic Corporation (Corines); Simon & Schuster, Inc. (Jonathan Newcomb); Esquire magazine (Whittle)—and from the political realm—Associate Counsel to the President (Christopher Cerf); member of the U.S. House of Representatives (Rev. Floyd Flake).

The most striking feature of the Edison board, however, is the prevalence of individuals from the investment, securities and banking industry. Ten executive officers have current or recent affiliations with the following companies: American Express (James Howland); Blue Rock Capital L.P. (Virginia Bonker); J.W. Childs Associates L.P. (John

Childs); UBS Capital Americas (Charles Delaney); J.P. Morgan Capital Corporation (John Fullerton); Investor Growth Capital Inc. (Klas Hillstrom); the Sprout Group (Robert Finzi, Janet Hickey); Leeds Equity Mangement L.L.C. (Jeffrey Leeds); and the Union Bank of Switzerland (Donald Sunderland).

With such seemingly high-powered management, how does the company measure up? Does Edison live up to its ambitious academic claims? Is the company a financial winner? The short answer to both questions is 'No.'

Edison's academic record

One of the few examinations of Edison's academic record, published by the American Federation of Teachers in 1998,[7] found "uneven quality and mixed results in raising student achievement," noting that the company's results fail to match the company's claims. According to the report, "Edison's reports and promotional materials often overstate their schools' success, and actual results are, at best, modest."

The report found that student performance in Edison schools is "mixed and inconclusive," and that accurate evaluation of the company's success is difficult because of "faulty baselines for comparison and incomplete test score information". It notes that Edison schools enjoy a number of potential advantages, including "a student body backed up by motivated parents; declining number of high-poverty students over time; [and] a longer school day and year...." The report also notes that Edison schools also enjoy a financial advantage, "spending more money per pupil than comparable public schools" and, in some cases, receiving extra funds from the public and from Edison investors. These potential advantages are offset, according to the report, by a number of shortcomings, including:

- "Edison cuts corners on [its commercial education program] jeopardizing [its]...effectiveness....
- Class size tends to be high.
- Edison relies heavily on inexperienced teachers.
- Teacher turnover in Edison schools is high.

Shortly after the AFT's report, researchers at Western Michigan University came to similar conclusions, after their analysis of a sample of ten Edison schools. "Our findings suggest that Edison student do not perform as well as Edison claims in its annual reports on student performance."[8]

These and other concerns about Edison's academic record have also become matters of broader public debate.

In mid-March, 2001, the San Francisco Board of Education moved to revoke the contract of the Edison Charter Academy. According to media reports, this move, which resulted in a 90-day notice to correct violations regarding unusually high teacher turnover,[9] followed allegations that Edison forced poorly performing students to attend other schools in order to keep the company's promise to raise test scores.[10]

In late March, 2001, parents at five of New York City's lowest-scoring public schools overwhelmingly voted against Edison's proposed takeover of these schools[11], which serve 4,800 students.[12]

In February, 2002, in response to "one of the most ambitious and controversial privatization projects in the history of U.S. education,"[13] U.S. Congressman Chaka Fattah released an extensive letter to members of the Philadelphia School Reform Commission, outlining a long list of concerns about Edison's academic record across the United States.[14]

In mid-May, 2002, Boston Renaissance Charter School, one of the first and best-known schools to contract with the company, terminated its contract with Edison. According to the president of the school, the contract, which would not have expired for another three years, was ended early in part because academic achievement at the school was lower than expected.[15]

Concerns about the academic performance of students at schools contracted to Edison, and Edison's claims about that performance, are unlikely to subside soon.

Edison's financial record

Edison's financial performance has been even worse. The company's stock prices have recently taken a severe battering, and Edison faces a raft of investor class action suits for allegedly issuing misleading financial information. Its financial future remains uncertain.[16]

In 2000, investment firm Smartmoney.com touted Edison as the "best play" in the private-sector education industry.[17] However, even then, some industry analysts remained skeptical that the company could make money and provide high-quality education:

> "So far, the bigger the company has grown, the more red ink it has spilled, with losses reaching nearly $50 million last year alone. Wall Street believes the company could be profitable by 2003, but only if it grows to about 300 schools, letting it spread its heavy central over head over many more students. 'If Edison's pace in signing new contracts slows, the whole thing will be dead in the water,' says one analyst."[18]

Indeed, in its offering prospectus, Edison states that "we have not yet demonstrated that public schools can be profitably managed by private companies, and we are not certain when we will become profitable, if at all."[19] According to Multex.com, "analysts expect the company to lose 88 cents per share on revenues of $377.2 million in fiscal 2001, and lose 71 cents per share on revenues of $553.8 million in fiscal 2002."[20]

For a time, despite these losses, many analysts hardly blinked, noting that an estimated $350 billion in taxpayers' dollars are channeled into primary and secondary education each year.[21] Their optimism was buoyed by President Bush's 2002 budget, which calls for "nearly a 12% hike in discretionary spending for the Education Department—the largest increase for any federal department. Most of that money would be used for increased testing, greater accountability, and broader flexibility for states and municipalities to implement custom-tailored turnaround measures. Edison Schools, naturally, would be all too happy to throw its hat into that ring and collect some of the Bush windfall in the process."[22]

However, Edison stock has dropped precipitously. After trading consistently above US$14 for most of the past year, and a high of $28 on June 6, 2001, it began a steep decline in late April 2002. As May came to an end, Edison stock was trading only marginally over $1. This descent followed news that, instead of managing all of the 45 Philadelphia schools slated for privatization, the company would only manage 20 of them.[23] Five prominent analysts subsequently downgraded Edison.[24]

But the bad news for the company ran deeper. An article published in February had revealed that Edison was boosting its revenue by counting "teachers' salaries and other expenses for school districts across the country as revenue, although Edison never receives it." The article quoted a former chief accountant of the Security and Exchange Commission (SEC) as saying, "I think the accounting is just wrong. Edison never gets the cash."[25] On May 14, it was confirmed that Edison had been the subject of an informal SEC inquiry into its financial record keeping practices and that the company had, as a result, agreed to alter its financial reporting[26]. The following day, three law firms, representing aggrieved investors, announced class action suits against Edison Schools for knowingly misrepresenting the company's revenues. Eight more similar suits were filed in the following two weeks. Many of the eleven also cite PricewaterhouseCooper, Edison's auditor, as a defendant.[27]

The Edison experience: the EMO as financial benefit for elite corporate executives

Whatever the future financial viability of Edison Schools, EMOs clearly have the potential to attract sophisticated American investors and use public funds to leverage significant amounts of private capital. However, the key lesson from the Edison experience may be that élite corporate operatives can derive stout personal benefits by managing companies that manage schools—using public resources.

During Edison's hard-fought but unsuccessful effort to obtain the right to manage five New York City schools earlier this year, Edison founder and chief executive H. Christopher Whittle attracted media attention by selling roughly 12% of his holdings in the company, worth nearly $US16 million.[28] According to documents required by the Securities and Exchange Commission, other Edison officers have also conducted hefty transactions[29]:

- Director John W. Childs, as 10% beneficial owner, acquired 2.7 million shares on March 16, 2001, and sold 868,000, the latter transaction netting $20 million in proceeds. In late December 2000, Childs personally gave away $518,000 worth of Edison shares as a gift.
- Chief Development Officer Manuel Rivera sold $1.8 million worth of Edison shares between August 8, 2000, and June 14, 2001.

- Chief Operating Officer Christopher Cerf acquired shares via his exercise of stock options for a paper gain of $273,000, and sold just under $1 million worth of shares, in late June 2001.
- Author and Edison Co-founder John Chubb acquired shares via exercise of stock options for a paper gain of nearly $1.3 million, and obtained proceeds of $623,000 from share sales, between August 8, 2000, and June 13, 2001.

Edison stock is highly concentrated. Edison's officers and directors, and entities affiliated with them, together own shares representing approximately 20% of the voting power of the class A common stock, 76% of the class B common stock, and 35% of the combined voting power of the company's class A and class B common stock. This gives them significant influence over the future direction of the company. H. Christopher Whittle, president and chief executive officer and a director, *alone* controls approximately 14%, 66% and 27% of voting power of the aforementioned types of stock.[30]

Edison officers and directors also receive significant compensation packages. John Chubb and Christopher Cerf were paid US$265,500 and $291,175, respectively, for the fiscal year ending June 30, 2001. Chairman of the Board Benno Schmidt, Jr. was paid $306,840, and H. Christopher Whittle $298,080.[31] One of the class action suits announced in late May alleges that, "despite massive investor losses," Whittle "paid himself more than $5 million annually and in one year alone cashed out stock options in excess of $15 million.... [O]ther top executives sold blocks of Edison Schools stock worth at least $5.5 million each."[32]

Whatever the future holds for Edison,[33] there is little question that for-profit education can provide healthy benefits for some private individuals and their corporate affiliates. It remains to be seen if companies like Edison Schools can take root in the United States. If they do, and if GATS rules restricting governments' regulatory ability[34] facilitate their expansion into other countries, EMOs could become very big business indeed—potentially at the expense not just of investors but of countless children around the world.

Endnotes

[1] Edison Schools, Inc., Profile, Business Summary, Yahoo! Finance, accessed May 30, 2002, available free online at http://biz.yahoo.com/p/e/edsn.html.

[2] The Edison Schools, Inc. website is http://www.edisonschools.com
[3] Ibid..
[4] Edison Schools, Inc., Business Description, Yahoo! Finance, p. 2, accessed May 2001. http://yahoo.marketguide.com/MGI/busidesc.asp?target=/stocks/companyinformation/busidesc&Ticker=EDSN.
[5] Sherrid, Pamela and Wildaysky, Ben, The ABCs of learning – and making money; Can the Edison Schools pull in profits?, *U.S. News*, November 22, 1999.
[6] The following information, reportedly current as of November 2000, is extracted from Business Information Database, Yahoo! Finance, op. cit..
[7] *Student Achievement in Edison Schools: Mixed Results in an Ongoing Enterprise*, American Federation of Teachers, May 7, 1998. (available at http://www.aft.org/research/edisonproject/support/pr.htm) In addition to this detailed report, this website also contains Edison's response to the AFT report published on the same date, together with a point-by-point rejoinder to Edison's critique which is dated June 15th.
[8] Miron, Gary and Applegate, Brooks, *An Evaluation of Student Achievement in Edison Schools Opened in 1995 and 1996*, Kalamazoo, The Evaluation Center, Western Michigan University, 2000. Cited in Bracey, 2002, op. cit., p. 9.
[9] Another Bush Victory, Farzad, Roben, Smartmoney.com, April 30, 2001, p. 3. http://www.yahoo.smartmoney.com)
[10] Higher Scores Aren't Cure-All, School Run for Profit Learns, Edward Wyatt, *New York Times*, March 13, 2001.
[11] Defeat Aside, Edison Plans to Expand, Edward Wyatt, *New York Times*, April 1, 2001. The Big City; Preferring the Devil They Know, John Tierney, *New York Times*, April 3, 2001.
[12] Business Information Database, op. cit.; Significant Developments, item for December 21, 2000.
[13] Privatizing the classroom: A plan to hand over the management of Philadelphia's 60 poorest-performing public schools to a for-profit company tomorrow has generated outrage in the city, Schmidt, Sarah, *National Post*, November 29, 2001, p. A16.
[14] SRC Notified on Edison's poor record of performance, U.S. Congressman Chaka Fattah, news release, February 4, 2002, available at http://www.house.gov/apps/list/speech/pa02_fattah/srcnotified.html .
[15] Charter school cuts ties with Edison, Lindsay, Jay, Associated Press, May 16, 2002. available at http://biz.yahoo.com/ap/020516/edison_schools_2.html.
[16] A continually updated chronological collation of business media stories about Edison is available free at http://biz.yahoo.com/n/e/edsn.html.
[17] See Another Bush Victory, op. cit..
[18] The ABCs of learning – and making money; Can the Edison Schools pull in profits?, op. cit.
[19] Edison Schools Files to Make Initial Offering, Joseph Pereira, *Wall Street Journal*, August 3, 1999. Cited in National Center for Policy Analysis, Edison Schools Inc. to Go Public (http://www.ncpa.org/pi/edu/pd080399d.html)
[20] Business Information Database, op. cit.
[21] Joseph Pereira, op. cit.
[22] Roben Farzad, op. cit.

[23] Some of the controversial events surrounding the Philadelphia privatization scheme are highlighted in Bracey, 2002, op. cit., pp. 7-9. See also: Edison Schools Announces Loss, Bergstrom, Bill, Associated Press, May 14, 2002, available online at http://biz.yahoo.com/ap/020514/edison_schools_2.html.

[24] The analysts and the dates of downgrading are: Gerard Klauer Mattison (18 April), Merrill Lynch (26 April), Bear Stearns (30 April), JP Morgan (1 May), and USB Piper Jaffray (9 May). Yahoo! Analyst Recommendations, available at http://biz.yahoo.com/c/e/edsn.html.

[25] Edison Schools Boost Revenue with Money it Never Receives, Bloomberg News, February 12, 2002.

[26] It is interesting to note that some financial observers have drawn links between the Edison case and the recent Enron scandal and point to its potential implications for other sectors. For example, according to Forbes' Dan Ackman, "in announcing the settlement, the SEC announced — or clarified – a disclosure policy that could have a wide impact on the energy trading industry, and perhaps beyond." He explains:

"Throughout its existence, Edison reported as revenue money that was used to pay salaries of teachers and others who remain employees of school districts, not of Edison. That money passes through Edison … on the way to the teachers, and was revenue to Edison in the sense that the company was paid the money as part of its management contract. But it was revenue in a fairly technical sense only. This method is known as 'gross' reporting of revenue.

Energy traders have taken to gross reporting of revenue with a vengeance. Indeed, of all the leading energy traders, only [one] reports net, rather than gross, revenue. This is how these companies grew—or appeared to grow—so quickly, even while the total end sales of energy and natural gas were increasing just marginally…

Sophisticated investors say that it doesn't matter whether revenue is reported on a gross or net basis, because profits are the same either way. One Wall Street analyst, who asked not to be identified, says he always understood the nature of the energy traders' revenue, and paid them no mind…. But others – including analysts – had no idea how the revenue was booked…

In the Edison case, the SEC said that reporting these funds as revenue did not violate Generally Accepted Accounting Principles. The SEC did find, though, that Edison committed violations by failing to provide accurate disclosure of the nature of its revenue…

[T]he SEC has raised a flag: Even if your reporting was technically accurate, it still may have been misleading and fraudulent. There could be many prosecutions down the road.

(With Edison case, SEC aims to teach a lesson, Ackman, Dan, Forbes.com, accessed May 30, 2002, available at http://www.forbes.com/2002/05/15/0515edison_print.html.)

[27] The announcements of these cases and, for some, supporting legal documents can be obtained at http://biz.yahoo.com/n/e/edsn.html , op. cit..

[28] Founder of Edison Schools Sells Some of His Stock in Company, Edward Wyatt, New York Times, March 23, 2001.

[29] The following Edison financial reports are available at http://biz.yahoo.com/t/e/edsn.html. The transactions noted in the text are current as of August 31, 2001.
[30] Edison Schools Inc (EDSN), Quarterly Report to the Security and Exchange Commission, SEC form 10-Q, available at http://biz.yahoo.com/e/l/e/edsn.html. This report also notes that "Mr. Whittle and WSI Inc., a corporation controlled by Mr. Whittle...have pledged to Morgan Guarantee Trust Company of New York all of their direct and indirect interests in Edison to secure personal obligations. These obligations become due in February 2003."
[31] The rates of compensation of Edison officers and directors may be found at http://yahoo.marketguide.com/MGI/compens.asp?nss=print&target=%2Fstocks%2Fcompanyinformation%2Fofficersanddirectors%2Fcompens&ticker=EDSN&rt=biograph. Whittle, together with some other Edison officials, reportedly receive other financial benefits; see Bracey, 2002, op. cit., p. 2.
[32] Investors file class-action lawsuit against Edison Schools, Inc., Berman DeValerio Pease Tabacco Burt & Pucillo Announces, Press Release, May 22, 2002. Available online at http://biz.yahoo.com/prnews/020522/new035_1.html.
The legal firm's complaint states (para 55):
"Despite massive investor losses, individual Defendants Whittle, Cerf and Field have reaped enormous financial profits from Edison stock. Upon information and belief, Defendant Whittle paid himself as much as $23 million in compensation and fees (more than $5 million annually) and throughout the Class Period had been systematically cashing out his stock options. In one year alone Defendant Whittle sold more than 650,000 shares of Edison stock for proceeds in excess of $15 million. Likewise, it has been reported that Defendants Cerf and Field have sold significant blocks of Edison stock at huge profits, each Defendant amassing a financial windfall of at least $4.5 million a piece (sic)."
[33] Edison counts a number of companies among its competitors, including: Beacon Education Management, Charter Schools USA, The Leona Group, Mosaica Education, Inc., National Heritage Academy SABIS Educational Systems, Bright Horizons Family Solutions and KIPP Academy, Inc.. http://yahoo.marketguide.com/MGI/busidesc.asp?target=/stocks/companyinformation/busidesc&Ticker=EDSN). Moreover, as Edison notes in its quarterly report to the US Government, "We expect the market for providing private, for-profit management of public schools will become increasingly competitive." Edison Schools Inc (EDSN), Quarterly Report, op. cit.
[34] The potential impact of the GATS on governments' ability to regulate, or re-regulate, the auditing and accounting sector gained media attention shortly after the recent debacle involving energy giant Enron and its auditor Arthur Andersen. In light of the alleged financial malpractice of Edison Schools and its auditor PricewaterhouseCoopers, this issue could also prove important for government regulation of EMOs. See, for example:
W.T.O. pact would set global accounting rules, DePalma, Anthony, *New York Times*, March 1, 2002; and
With Edison case, SEC aims to teach a lesson, op. cit..

3.2 In brief: the impacts of commercialization and privatization

In cataloguing the various types of commercialization and privatization, it is possible to lose sight of the main issue: that these developments are eroding the core values and aims of public education systems.

Public education is designed to be affordable, accessible, and universal, and hence is a key component of democratic society. As the Canadian Coalition for Public Education has noted,[36] public education prepares students to be active participants in society. Students not only learn to read, write, think critically, analyze, work with numbers, use technology, and learn employment skills, but they also learn to communicate, to understand, to respect different points of view, and to cooperate with people from diverse social, ethnic and economic backgrounds. Public education systems are also responsive to students and citizens (public institutions accommodate the diverse interests, abilities, and learning styles of students), are accountable to the community, and open to public scrutiny.

Commercializing public education tends to promote narrower interests, and undermines the fundamental principles of equity, diversity, and openness upon which public education systems are based—some of the same principles that are also enshrined in the Universal Declaration of Human Rights, considered in Chapter 1.

3.3 Clash of principles: GATS vs. the public education system

There are underlying tensions between the widely recognized aims of public education and the principles of the GATS. Instead of seeing universal access to quality public education as a crucial investment in the social and economic health of any democracy, the GATS treats education as just another service sector potentially available for commercial exploitation. By consolidating and augmenting pressures for commercialization and privatization (see below), the GATS undermines public education's central principles of affordability, accessibility, and universality.

On a practical level, the GATS adds to the administrative burdens already faced by local school boards and higher levels of government. It places the expensive onus on these bodies to ensure that their current and future activities are consistent with complex, arcane international rules that will change frequently and are explicitly designed to become increasingly restrictive.

Finally, in contrast to the obvious accountability of local and regional school boards to local citizens, the GATS establishes—particularly through its dispute settlement process—a mechanism of administration that is opaque, distant, and only very indirectly accountable to ordinary citizens. In each of these ways, the GATS conflicts with the basic principles underlying public education systems.

3.3.1 Education policies that are deemed to be "barriers to trade" are targeted in GATS negotiations

On a practical level, GATS proponents have described broad categories of policy measures that, in their view, violate the principles of the treaty. Many of these so-called "barriers to trade" exist in the education sector even if they do not, at least for now, violate existing GATS rules or commitments. A review of what GATS proponents consider GATS-inconsistent "barriers to trade" therefore provides valuable insights into those education policies that are likely to come under more direct threat, both in current and subsequent negotiations, to expand the reach of the GATS.

In a paper prepared in 1999 for an international services conference, OECD Trade Directorate official Rachel Thompson presented a list of trade barriers, which were applicable to all service sectors, that could be collated according to their trade-restrictiveness and used to set "benchmarks" for further liberalization.[37] This "indicative 'reference list' of cross sectoral measures" includes many measures that could apply to the education sector. It includes the following:

- "Requirement to obtain authorization, licence or permit in order to market or supply services.
- Commercial presence in country required, and granted only to specified 'brand-name' entities.
- Requirement to use specified network access or connection provider.
- Requirement that personal or commercial data is not to be transferred out of the country in which it was generated, without specifying the policy reasons for the restriction or permitting transfer subject to adherence to reasonable standards.
- Scope of foreign business limited to specified activities, narrower than those permitted local firms.
- Approval of foreign investment required, based on economic needs test or 'net national benefit.'
- Case-by-case authorization at political level with ceilings on permitted foreign investment varying by sector or within sectors; without clear, consistently applied criteria for approval.
- Licencing, authorization to provide [services] granted only to companies permitted to establish, with licences limited numerically or subject to significant limitations on foreign equity participation, employment, or specified number of local staff, etc.

- Permission [for temporary entry/stay of service providers] subject to passing local examination to be recognized as professional or specialist.
- Requirement to complete or undertake further training in the host country in order to be recognized as professional or specialist.
- Requirement that a specified proportion of foreign staff have local understudies for training/transfer of skills."

A similar list of "trade barriers"—focusing specifically on education—was subsequently compiled in a report to the Asia-Pacific Economic Cooperation (APEC) Group on Services, which had identified education services as a priority sector for action. This report, which was published in 2000, was prepared under the direction of the Australian and New Zealand Ministries of Education and Foreign Affairs and Trade. It identifies policy measures that affect trade and investment in education services, including K-12 education (see sidebar).[38]

The APEC compilation of so-called "barriers to trade" in education is far more than a mere academic exercise. The report in which this collation emerges appears to serve as the principal reference for both New Zealand[39] and Australia's[40] formal GATS negotiating proposals. The Australian proposal, for example, issued in late 2001, cites the report and refers to such measures as "impediments to further liberalization of the education services sector."[41] It sidesteps the policy concerns identified in the original APEC paper, proposing simply that the first principle for education service negotiations should be "access to the best education services wherever they are provided and through whatever mode of supply they are provided"[42] and that the GATS negotiations should not prevent the application of regulatory measures that are "necessary"

"Barriers to Trade" in education			
Cross-border trade	Consumption abroad	Commercial presence	Presence of natural persons
• Requirements to authorize payments of fees for education services • Measures affecting: 　• Import or export of educational material 　• Import or export of distance education services 　• Access to the provision of services via electronic media	From the perspective of the host economy: • Visa entry requirements and costs • Quota on international students • Quotas on students at a particular institution • Rules on sectors in which foreign students are not allowed to enrol • Rules on student access to employment in the host economy • Foreign currency requirements for foreign students • Extent of recognition of prior educational qualifications • Recognition of qualifications issued in other economies From the perspective of the home economy: • Requirements for students to obtain exit visas from home economy • Home economy rules on access to foreign exchange	• Requirement for foreign providers to satisfy an economic needs test • Limits on foreign equity • Requirements on forms of commercial relationships • Measures specifying the legal structure of providers • Nationality or residence requirements for permanent staff • Special tax obligations	• Quotas on the number of temporary staff • Other measures affecting entry or stay of foreign staff • Labour market measures applied to visiting staff • Nationality or residence requirements

Reproduced from:
Table 1, "Summary of policy measures", *Measures affecting trade and investment in education services in the Asia-Pacific region*, A report to the APEC Group on Services 2000, APEC Secretariat, December, 2000. (available online at www.apecsec.org.sg/)

to achieve education policy objectives. The Australian proposal also appears—obliquely—to open the door to public subsidies being granted to foreign for-profit education service providers on an equivalent basis to domestic public, non-profit providers, stating simply that the negotiations should not prevent members from "providing public funds for education".[43]

In its December 2000 proposal to other GATS members, the United States identifies a number of government measures, which it characterizes as "obstacles," that it requests all WTO members review as they consider undertaking further GATS commitments in education.

Seen from the point of view of education policy, these so-called "obstacles" to trade are more appropriately understood as domestic policy instruments that could reasonably be required to meet legitimate educational policy objectives. Regulations governing joint partnerships and local hiring, for instance, could be required to ensure that programs have an appropriate level of Canadian content. Subsidy programs for adult education and training, which are typically complex and tailored to the needs of communities and the characteristics of local providers, could easily run afoul of seemingly innocuous rules on transparency. Negotiating GATS rules to remove or reduce these "obstacles," as the U.S. proposes, would increasingly restrict the ability of governments to regulate in the education sector.

These lists of "obstacles to trade" provide important clues to the intentions of influential GATS members in the current round of negotiations and, specifically, the degree to which education services are on the negotiating table. For example, the U.S. proposal does not pertain to K-12 education, but is limited to higher education, adult education, and training. However, many of the "obsta-

United States: Education "obstacles" for review in GATS negotiations

Obstacles in this sector
- Prohibition of higher education, adult education, and training services offered by foreign entities.
- Lack of an opportunity for foreign suppliers of higher education, adult education, and training services to obtain authorization to establish facilities within the territory of the Member country.
- Lack of an opportunity for foreign suppliers of higher education, adult education, and training services to qualify as degree granting institutions.
- Inappropriate restrictions on electronic transmission of course materials.
- Economic needs test on suppliers of these services.
- Measures requiring the use of a local partner.
- Denial of permission for private sector suppliers of higher education, adult education, and training to enter into and exit from joint ventures with local or nonlocal partners on a voluntary basis.
- Where government approval is required, exceptionally long delays are encountered and, when approval is denied, no reasons are given for the denial and no information is given on what must be done to obtain approval in the future.
- Tax treatment that discriminates against foreign suppliers.
- Foreign partners in a joint venture are treated less favourably than the local partners.
- Franchises are treated less favourably than other forms of business organization.
- Domestic laws and regulations are unclear and administered in an unfair manner.
- Subsidies for higher education, adult education, and training are not made known in a clear and transparent manner.
- Minimum requirements for local hiring are disproportionately high, causing uneconomic operations.

> - Specialized, skilled personnel (including managers, computer specialists, expert speakers) needed for a temporary period of time, have difficulty obtaining authorization to enter and leave the country.
> - Repatriation of earnings is subject to excessively costly fees and/or taxes for currency conversion.
> - Excessive fees/taxes are imposed on licensing or royalty payments.
>
> Reproduced from:
> World Trade Organization, Council for Trade in Services, Special Session, *Communication from the United States, Higher (Tertiary) Education, Adult Education and Training*, 18 December 2000, S/CSS/W/23, para. 10.

cles" it lists could apply equally to measures affecting K-12 education, and nations that have already made commitments in this area could face increased pressure to agree to a comparable level of liberalization in primary and secondary education.

Both the U.S. and New Zealand proposals dwell on seemingly obscure classification issues—the former emphasizing that testing services apply to education at all levels, the latter proposing that student recruitment and placement services should be classified as education services. The explicit incorporation of what are often commercial services reinforce the observation made by the WTO Secretariat that "the separation of public and private domains [is] not always clear."[44]

More significantly, unlike the U.S. proposal, the Australian proposal is not limited to higher education; it includes secondary education and does not exclude primary education. Neither is it limited to private education. This proposal thus offers compelling evidence that public policy measures concerning *secondary* education—as opposed to *higher* education[45]—are now squarely on the GATS negotiating table.

These GATS proposals echo the general proposals made by the private, corporate-led Global Services Network, which, in the run-up to start of GATS 2000 negotiations, called for the WTO negotiations on services to be used "to achieve a contestable, competitive market in every services sector in every WTO member country."[46]

3.4 Some impacts of the GATS, and of commercialization and privatization, are mutually reinforcing

Some impacts of the treaty are inextricably linked to the effects of commercialization and privatization. As discussed in the following sections, these are positive, mutually-reinforcing interactions. On the one hand, increased commercialization and privatization extend the reach of GATS rules and increase the domestic pressure for future expansion of the treaty. On the other hand, the treaty generates unrelenting pressure for greater commercialization and privatization.

3.4.1 Increased commercialization and privatization leads to greater GATS coverage, both directly and indirectly.

Direct expansion of GATS coverage

As previously discussed, in order for services to be outside the reach of the treaty, they must not be commercial and must not be in competition with other services or providers. The size of this set of excluded services, while almost certainly smaller than generally recognized, remains controversial. What cannot reasonably be contested, however, is that, when a public service is commercialized or privatized, it acquires, by definition, a commercial aspect. Hence, a newly-commercialized service *necessarily* falls outside the governmental authority exclusion and so is covered by applicable GATS rules. That is, private, for-profit education *by definition* is commercial and hence covered by GATS. Where standardized student testing is contracted by a province to a commercial firm, for example, this testing service would become a commercial education service, thereby falling unequivocally within the scope of the GATS.[47]

Indirect expansion of GATS coverage
Increased commercialization and privatization also leads indirectly to greater GATS coverage. For example, commercializing a particular service often opens up many new prospects for other services and providers to be deemed to be "in competition with" the commercialized service. These services, even if they have and continue to be provided publicly on a non-commercial basis, may now be deemed to be "in competition with" the newly-commercialized service. As a result, these public services—which otherwise would arguably remain protected by the government authority exclusion[48]—could lose their excluded status merely as a result of another service being commercialized.

It is self-evident that commercializing a service removes it from the safety of the government authority exclusion. What is not immediately obvious is that commercializing a service in itself can have the effect of dragging *other* public, non-commercial services out of the protective government authority 'lifeboat' where these services would otherwise have remained safe from GATS rules. Such indirect expansion of GATS coverage could be far-reaching. As international trade lawyers recently noted in a legal opinion,[49] according to GATS Article I:3(c),

"service providers do not have to be 'like' service providers or provide 'like' services to be in competition with one another. To be in competition, they could simply 'try to get what others also seek.' It could also be argued that competition may take place between providers irrespective of the mode of supply. For instance, a service provider delivering a course through the Internet could be in competition with a provider delivering the same course through a regular classroom."

According to this analysis, a non-profit, publicly-provided classroom education course that itself remained non-commercial could nevertheless lose its excluded status if another service, provided over the Internet, were commercialized and subsequently deemed by a WTO dispute panel to be "in competition with" the public education classroom course in question.[50] This indirect effect thus has the potential to extend the reach of the GATS farther into the heart of public service systems.[51]

Hypothetical example
The potential for unintended GATS coverage of public services
Country 'A' agrees to apply the GATS national treatment and market access provisions to secondary math courses delivered to its citizens commercially on the Internet. A commercial education provider, based in another WTO country 'B,' demands the same government subsidy that is provided to a consortium of public school boards offering 'distance education' math courses over the Internet, on a non-commercial basis. The company persuades its home country to support its export expansion bid by mounting a GATS challenge on the company's behalf.
Country 'A' defends its domestic distance education math courses on the basis that they are "services provided in the exercise of governmental authority" and so excluded

from the GATS. A GATS dispute panel rejects the country's claim, ruling that the distance education math course is "in competition with" the commercial math course and hence not covered by the governmental authority exclusion.

The panel also rules that supplemental fees for materials, together with hidden cross-subsidization, render the distance education course a "commercial" venture—making it fully subject to the GATS market access and national treatment obligations undertaken by country 'A.' Faced with having to pay equivalent subsidies to all foreign, for-profit providers, the cash-strapped public school boards in country 'A' withdraw their distance education math course, thereby ceding the "market" to the foreign commercial provider.

In a separate case, another foreign, for-profit Internet provider of math courses demands an adjusted per-pupil subsidy on the basis that a subsidy is provided to public institutions offering similar, competing courses that are taught by regular teachers in ordinary classrooms. In the resulting GATS dispute, the panel rules that the public school courses do indeed compete with those provided commercially over the Internet and so are not excluded from GATS rules. However, the panel rejects the company's claim for an adjusted, equivalent subsidy, ruling that the classroom course is not "commercial" and is not "like" the Internet course, so is not covered by country 'A's national treatment commitments, which are limited to commercial education.

Just because a particular public service does not benefit from the governmental authority exclusion does not mean, of course, that it is subject to the most demanding GATS obligations; this depends upon what specific commitments each WTO member makes. However, a specific commitment regarding any service—even a service that is obviously commercial—that could conceivably be interpreted as being in competition with public education services, renders those public education services 'hostages to fortune.' Critically, in the absence of clear definitions in the text, what aspect of public service systems are deemed to be "in competition with" another service or service provider will ultimately be determined not by member governments, but by appointed trade panelists, based solely on GATS rules and international law. Thus, the protection of the relevant public service from the specific commitment in question depends in part upon a GATS dispute panel rendering a narrow interpretation of "competition," which, on its face, is a rather unlikely prospect. Moreover, where a panel deems the public service to be in competition with the committed commercial service, that public service could fall outside the protective governmental authority exclusion and, if it is deemed to be "like" its committed counterpart (see below), be subject to the same specific commitment. In short, *a non-profit public service could, merely through the determination of a dispute panel, become subject to a specific commitment that the member intended to apply only to a commercial service.*

In principle, it may be possible for members that are alert to this danger to exercise cautious foresight by carefully defining and specifying all of the various aspects of their public service systems that are to be protected from each specific commitment they make. However, the treaty applies to all types of service delivery (including services delivered via the internet) and makes no explicit allowance for members to distinguish, in their specific commitments, between public and private, or between non-profit or for-profit, delivery.[52] But even if such an approach were permissible, and it may be, it would be an exceedingly difficult and complicated task to ensure complete, comprehensive protection for public service systems in this way.[53] A similar approach to provincial and state reservations under NAFTA proved so unwieldy that it was eventually abandoned in favour of a general, albeit limited, reservation for sub-national measures. The fact that Canada has already made a significant scheduling mistake in the GATS[54] and has unexpectedly lost other WTO cases makes any Canadian government assurance that public services will remain fully protected through such a complex process less than convincing.

From the standpoint of safeguarding Canada's public education system from GATS rules, it is clearly preferable to refrain from making *any* specific commitments involving or affecting education, including commitments that are limited to commercial education services. This approach remains a realistic and viable negotiating option. Unfortunately, there is evidence that Canadian officials are preparing precisely the action that seems so risky—making specific commitments in "education" (presumably commercial education services)—while purporting to protect "public education." This disturbing prospect is considered later, in Chapter 5.

3.4.2 Increased commercialization and privatization increases domestic pressure for GATS expansion

Increased commercialization and privatization create a distinct constituency that is generally predisposed to open services markets, both domestically and in foreign markets. Together with export-oriented public entities, commercial education service providers can be expected to apply pressure on the Canadian government to obtain GATS concessions from other countries in their target markets wherever this is seen to be commercially advantageous.

There is considerable interest in Canada—from commercial companies, public institutions, and governments—in increasing exports of education services. The Government of Canada website highlights the government's public commitment to "promoting the export of Canadian educational services." It notes, for example, that "close to 100 participants from the education sector formed the largest single contingent on the recent Team Canada mission to China."[55] The Department of Foreign Affairs and International Trade also maintains an online resource centre designed to "assist the Canadian knowledge industry to promote and export its products and services effectively in international markets."[56]

The federal government also contributed financial resources to bring the World Education Market to Vancouver in May 2001. The World Education Market (WEM) is an annual trade show "dedicated to the international business of education, training, and lifelong learning" that drew delegates from 930 organizations from 62 countries. As its promotional material for the 2002 trade show in Lisbon states, WEM brings together the leaders, decision-makers, and top executives from public and private sectors—as it puts it: "the pioneers who are shaping the education marketplace."[57]

For their part, some provincial governments also appear intent on fostering commercial or export education. The recently-elected government of British Columbia, for example, has introduced changes to the province's *School Act* to facilitate the formation, by school boards, of companies to purchase or provide educational services.[58]

Pressure from these commercial education providers can be expected to increase the momentum for expanding the GATS. Over time, this pressure is likely to rebound— increasing the pressure on the Canadian government for liberalization of the Canadian education "market" when other countries demand corresponding commitments on behalf of their commercial providers. The presence of foreign commercial providers within Canada's education sector could also spur education deregulation in this country. Direct deregulation of the sector is politically sensitive. However, similar deregulation can be achieved indirectly, with fewer political risks, through the GATS. Since the GATS process is complex and hidden from public view, commercialization and deregulation can be achieved out of the public eye, in ways that appear to be inadvertent or that have demonstrable benefits to some Canada-based service providers.[59]

3.4.3 The GATS exerts unrelenting pressure for greater commercialization and privatization

GATS proponents frequently claim that the GATS does not force member countries to commercialize services. For example, the WTO Secretariat has stated that "[t]here is no obligation on any WTO Member to allow foreign supply of any particular service—nor even to guarantee domestic competition."[60] It is true that the GATS does not *force* governments to privatize public services. However, as pointed out in a systematic rebuttal to the WTO claims about the GATS[61], by mandating repeated rounds of renegotiations to expand the reach of the treaty, the GATS exerts constant, unrelenting pressure to open services to foreign commercial providers. In these negotiations, every service is, in principle, perpetually on the negotiating table.

The GATS also helps consolidate commercialization wherever it occurs through the universally applicable Most Favoured Nation (MFN) rule (see below). Moreover, in practical terms, the treaty impedes governments' ability, where commitments are made, from restoring, revitalizing, or expanding public services. In these ways, the GATS intensifies pressure that already exists to commercialize and privatize public education services.

3.5 The GATS – at it now exists – contains specific threats to public education systems

Most countries consider education to be a fundamental entitlement of its citizens, critical for human, social and economic development. Largely because of this, the sector has been treated with greater caution; under the current version of the treaty, the education services sector is among the least committed sector in the GATS.[62] Education services are among the least threatened by the most restrictive GATS rules. Consequently, there is ample opportunity for members to prevent GATS national treatment and market access rules from applying to the sector; and efforts to achieve this are likely to be both timely and effective.

This comparatively good news must be balanced with the recognition that there is a general lack of understanding, among both governments and public education advocates, of the significant risks that already exist in the GATS. The GATS already curtails governments' ability to regulate the education sector in the public interest, a fact that has been obscured by proponents' misleading claims to the contrary.[63] Before examining the threats posed by the proposed expansion of the treaty, this analysis now turns to some of the particular GATS threats that the existing treaty already poses for public education.

3.5.1 GATS general obligations already apply to education

As noted above, a number of GATS general obligations are universal and unconditional; they apply 'across-the-board' to all services including education services—even where members have not made specific commitments in the sector.

Most favoured nation (MFN) treatment; an underrated obligation

While the Most Favoured Nation treatment rule is a long-established principle in treaties governing trade in goods, its transposition to services is quite problematic. It has already been shown to be a powerful obligation in two recent cases (EC Bananas and the Auto Pact), where it was interpreted forcefully, much to the apparent surprise of the European and Canadian governments, whose measures were attacked successfully.

The MFN rule requires that the best treatment granted to any foreign service or provider be extended to all like foreign services and service providers. The rule is sometimes encapsulated by the phrase, "if you favour one, you must favour all." On its face, the provision appears uncontroversial, even banal, requiring governments merely to treat Finnish companies the same as Mexican companies, for example. However, MFN is better understood as, in effect, a Most Favoured Corporation rule.[64] That is, a member government that grants one foreign corporation a regulatory or funding advantage must grant all such corporations the equivalent advantage immediately and unconditionally.

In practical terms, this has the potential to turn a modest market opening policy experiment from a rivulet into a torrent. Aside from the GATS legal implications of violating this GATS rule, this provision also adds to the political pressure on governments not to withdraw any such measures. Government would face opposition not from a single corporation, but from a powerful bloc of many corporations, each having commercial interests in gaining market access in the sector.

Hypothetical examples
MFN: potential pressure to turn market opening rivulets into floods?

    A provincial government in country 'A' grants a foreign corporation the ability to manage certain schools in a public school district. A corporation from a third country seeks the ability to manage certain schools in another public school district in the same province. Could the province's refusal of the company's application constitute a GATS MFN violation by country 'A'?

    A provincial government grants a Japan-based corporation a financial incentive to provide Japanese language instruction, in the classroom, to English-speaking students. A German corporation seeks the same incentive to provide classroom instruction in German. Would refusal constitute an MFN violation?

    A Mexican corporation seeks the same incentive to provide language instruction over the Internet. Would refusal constitute an MFN violation?

    A Japanese corporation seeks a financial incentive from Country 'A' to provide Japanese language instruction, *in Japan*, in a classroom, to English-speaking students from Country 'A'. Would refusal to provide the equivalent incentive constitute an MFN violation?

These questions cannot be answered definitively. At root, they are based on issues that are critical to the application of the GATS MFN obligation.[65] Firstly, to what extent should services and service suppliers operating in different modes be interpreted as "like" services? Secondly, is the electronic delivery of services covered by the GATS? Thirdly, should the electronically delivered services be interpreted as "like" services delivered non-electronically *within a particular mode of supply*? Fourthly, should electronically delivered services be interpreted as "like" services delivered non-electronically *in any of the four traditional modes of supply*?

WTO members have grappled with these complex legal issues for some time, without formally reaching a final consensus. However, it is generally agreed that the GATS applies "to all services regardless of the means of technology by which they are delivered."[66] Moreover, according to the WTO Secretariat, the following issues are areas where general agreement among members[67] exists:

- "The electronic delivery of services falls within the scope of the GATS, since the Agreement applies to all services regardless of the means by which they are delivered, and electronic delivery can take place under any of the four modes of supply. Measures affecting the electronic delivery of services are measures affecting trade in services and would therefore be covered by GATS obligations.
- The technological neutrality of the Agreement would also mean that electronic supply of services is permitted by specific commitments unless the schedule states otherwise.
- All GATS provisions, whether relating to general obligations (e.g., MFN, transparency, domestic regulation, competition, payments and transfer, etc.) or specific commitments (Market Access, National Treatment, or Additional Commitments), are applicable to the supply of services through electronic means."[68]

Discussions have also centred on the scope of MFN obligations with regard to the four modes of supply. In these deliberations, it has been noted that "the extent to which services and service suppliers operating in different modes could be considered "like" remains unclear." In particular, Brazil has correctly noted that two fundamentally different interpretations of the existing treaty text are possible[69]:

"First, likeness could be interpreted without regard to the mode of supply, i.e., on the basis of the nature of the economic activity performed regardless of the territorial presence of the supplier and the consumer. Such an interpretation drew on the jurisprudence established in the area of trade in goods, which defined likeness in terms of the essential characteristics of products.

The second possible interpretation would hold that MFN and national treatment applied within each mode of supply individually, based on a comparison of service suppliers that operate in "like circumstances." This second interpretation drew on another approach to likeness identified in jurisprudence on trade in goods, which was to define it on the basis of the "aims and effects" or of the regulatory objective being pursued by a certain measure affecting the product or its producers. In this connection, services and/or service suppliers would be considered "like" only if they were subject to the same regulatory framework, which did not mean that they necessarily had to be in compliance with the same regulatory framework. In practice, likeness would become a function of the mode of supply, being defined only within each mode individually."

With respect to the implications of electronically delivered services, the WTO Secretariat reports that:
"the issue of likeness is central to the application of MFN and...the main question to be addressed in this regard is whether electronically delivered services and those delivered by other methods should be considered "like services".... [T]here is considerable GATT jurisprudence which establishes that *the determination of likeness can only be made on a case-by-base basis.*"[70]

Finally, when it comes to market access and national treatment obligations, it is the general view among members that:
"the means of delivery does not alter specific commitments.... [These specific commitments] cover the supply of services through electronic means *unless otherwise specified.*"[71]

What all of this boils down to is that, within the *existing* treaty, the GATS MFN rule, coupled with the treaty's treatment of electronic delivery of services, could prove very problematic for public education and other public service systems[72]. It constitutes a potentially powerful tool by which foreign countries, acting on behalf of their domestic firms, could seek equivalent access, incentives and other advantages granted to any single foreign service provider. It remains unclear how these issues will ultimately be resolved. What is clear is that, in the absence of action by GATS members, these fundamental aspects of the treaty will be determined not by governments, but by appointed dispute panellists—and then on a case-by-case basis. If these panelists interpret the existing GATS provisions expansively, the electronic delivery of education services could transform market-opening rivulets in the sector into a liberalization flood.[73]

Transparency: introducing new administrative burdens, delineating future GATS targets

As noted in the previous chapter, GATS transparency rules require members to publish all measures, at all levels of government, that "pertain to or affect the operation" of the treaty. It also requires members to establish enquiry points and to inform the WTO Council for Trade in Services of any changes or new measures that "significantly affect trade in services" within sectors covered by members specific commitments. For most school boards and provincial governments, these requirements will come as a surprise. Unused to even considering the potential for challenges under international rules, they generally have neither the financial resources nor the expertise to vet their practices to determine if they conform to the complex maze of GATS rules. It can be expected that most will defer to the senior levels of government or, more probably, given the potential of a crippling GATS challenge, simply avoid or abandon any practices that could conceivably be seen as GATS-inconsistent. While the transparency provision may thus not appear to be particularly onerous, it is likely to cast a regulatory chill through public education systems and reinforce the already dominant position of federal trade ministries in Canada and elsewhere.

Hypothetical example

Transparency provisions 'flush out' soft drink advertising restrictions in schools

Concerned about growing commercialization, and eager to foster healthier diets among its students, a public school board in Country 'A' prohibits soft drink vending machines within its schools and notifies all other boards in the province of its action. As part of the GATS process of identifying measures that "pertain or affect the operation of the treaty," trade officials from Country 'A' canvass their provincial counterparts. Discovering the boards new policy, the officials include the measure in the list it submits to the Council for Trade in Services. Two major soft drinks companies based in the United States lobby their government to ensure that the measure is eliminated as a violation of the GATS market access commitments that Country 'A' has already made in the *advertising services* and *distribution services* sectors. Failing that, the companies lobby the U.S. government to obtain new specific commitments from Country 'A' in these areas that would roll back the restrictions on soft drink vending machines.[74]

The transparency provisions are also a powerful mechanism for exposing education measures, taken at any level, that violate the treaty or whose conformity is questionable. Through domestic reviews and, more formally, through the GATS requirement for reporting such measures, this provision draws attention to existing and proposed measures that may violate the treaty; it puts them 'up in lights,' making them more susceptible to elimination, in response to pressure brought to bear in future negotiating rounds.[75] The importance of transparency has recently been emphasized by Australian academics Tony Warren and Christopher Findlay:[76]

"Transparency of policy affecting services trade and investment is critical for successful reform. More information, in terms of the detail of policy and the analysis of its effects, helps mobilize the key countervailing interests against the protectionist forces in domestic economies, facilitates the construction of coalitions for reform by political leaderships, and adds to policy maker confidence...."[77]

Domestic regulation: the sword of Damocles
The GATS domestic regulation provisions hang, like the sword of Damocles, over public education and other public services. As previously discussed,[78] negotiations are currently under way in Geneva to fulfill the mandate, previously agreed by members, to "develop any necessary disciplines" to ensure that government measures do not constitute "unnecessary barriers to trade in services." Such new restrictions are intended to apply to "measures relating to qualification requirements ... technical standards and licensing requirements". The scope of these concepts remains unclear; however, each is likely to be broadly interpreted and so be of direct significance to public education.

Public education systems have yet to feel the direct impact of new domestic regulation rules, since no such rules have yet been negotiated.[79] The effect of the GATS domestic regulation provisions, as they now exist, are now indirect and difficult to ascertain. The direct effects, which could prove profound, depend upon the outcome of current negotiations.

Hypothetical example
   Domestic Regulation provision casts chill over proposed education regulations
   A province within Country 'A' embarks on a province-wide consultation process to determine how the public education system could better facilitate increased understanding among First Nations students, a rapidly-growing immigrant student population, and other students. A panel of

elected representatives and citizens concludes that the provincial qualification process for teachers entering the province from elsewhere should be bolstered to include courses on local First Nations history and on Asian history, to better address this issue. The panel also concludes that all curricula in use in the province, whatever its origins, should be modified accordingly, and that evidence of efforts to augment cross-cultural understanding should be a condition of licensing of schools.

Upon learning of the panel's conclusions, federal trade officials, intent on ensuring that no new trade barriers develop during sensitive GATS negotiations, add qualification requirements, technical standards, and licensing requirements to the list of inter-provincial trade barriers slated for reduction in ongoing negotiations on the little-known Canadian Agreement on Internal Trade (AIT). Responding to media inquiries about the purported economic cost of internal trade barriers, the provincial trade minister publicly states that the province will not introduce any new barriers. The panel's report is never implemented.

Monopolies and exclusive service suppliers: provisions in which public education could be threatened by specific commitments in commercial education?

The GATS restrictions on monopolies are hybrid provisions, combining both unconditional and conditional obligations. They specifically "apply to cases of exclusive service suppliers, where a member formally or in effect, a) authorizes or establishes a small number of service suppliers and b) substantially prevents competition among those suppliers in its territory."[80] The WTO rightly characterizes the treaty's Article VIII obligations as requiring each member to "ensure that any monopoly or exclusive supplier of a service in its territory acts in a manner consistent with that Member's obligations under Article II (MFN) and specific commitments."[81] These provisions thus have the effect of plugging a potential loophole; they make doubly certain that a country cannot evade its MFN and specific commitments simply through the operation of monopolies and exclusive service suppliers.

The effect of applying MFN and specific commitments to monopolies and exclusive service suppliers has not received much public attention or analysis.[82] In the education sector, it is not even clear what bodies constitute exclusive service suppliers. It would appear, however, that the licensing of schools for purposes of public financing and the certification of teachers fall within this category, as these are activities in which a member establishes a "small number of service suppliers...and substantially prevents competition among those suppliers." Even the delivery of classroom education itself could be interpreted as delivery by an "exclusive service supplier" and hence subject to the GATS monopoly rules. More specifically, provincial legislation specifying that, where a union has been certified, membership in that union is a condition of employment could be interpreted as establishing the union as an exclusive service supplier.[83]

A full examination of the potential impact of the GATS monopolies provisions is clearly warranted. What is clear from an initial appraisal, however, is that these provisions could be an important means through which specific commitments in private, commercial education could lead to new GATS threats to public education systems. Where a government makes specific commitments covering private education, for example, this could elicit complaints that public school boards are abusing their monopoly position. The prospect of the Canadian government making specific commitments for private education in just this way makes a detailed examination of this threat a matter of some urgency.

Hypothetical example
According to GATS rules, are public education boards "abusing" their monopoly rights?
Country 'A' fully covers "commercial" K-12 education services and service providers in its GATS specific commitments, asserting publicly that it has protected its "public" education system from GATS rules. One year later, a foreign commercial provider complains that the public education providers in Country 'A' are abusing their monopoly position. In its subsequent GATS complaint, Country 'B' argues on behalf of the commercial provider that Country 'A' is allowing its education providers to use their facilities, staff and infrastructure outside their monopoly areas to leverage their monopoly position, unfairly competing in courses also supplied by commercial education providers.

Despite the fact that Country 'A' clearly meant to protect its public education boards from the reach of the treaty, a GATS panel, not County 'A', determines to what extent these boards are subject to the GATS monopoly rules.

3.5.2. There are as yet few GATS specific commitments in education-related services

Canada has made no specific commitments in the education services sector as delineated in the CPC classification system described above[84]. As a result, as previously noted, the treaty's national treatment and market access rules—among the most onerous of GATS rules—do not now apply directly to the core of the Canadian public education system. (There are some commitments for services that apply to aspects of, or relate closely to, the public education system; a selection of these is considered in the following chapter.)

This absence of specific commitments means that all levels of government in Canada so far retain a considerable degree of public policy flexibility in the sector—a fundamental point that should not be overlooked. The degree to which this flexibility will be preserved, and Canada's education and other public service systems protected, is one of the most crucial facets of the GATS re-negotiation process that is now underway in Geneva.

Chapter 4
Future threats:
Negotiations to expand the GATS

While the existing treaty, together with increasing commercialization, entails significant risks, the negotiations that are now under way to expand the GATS pose the gravest threats to public education systems.

> "No sector will be excluded, and the aim must be, in no more than three years, to conclude an ambitious package of additional liberalization...in politically difficult as well as in other sectors."
> —Leon Brittan[1], *Towards GATS 2000 – A European Strategy*, June 2, 1998.
>
> "The WTO negotiations on services should be used to achieve a contestable, competitive market in every service sector in every WTO member country."
> —Global Services Network, *Statement on WTO Negotiations on Services*, November, 1999, p. 1.

4.1 The risks of an ever-expanding treaty

The GATS is an extraordinarily ambitious agreement. In addition to its exceptionally broad scope and coverage, discussed above, the treaty contains powerful, legally enforceable obligations that are backed up by trade sanctions. But the treaty contains another feature that is particularly critical for the future of public education. It has built into its very structure an overarching commitment for repeated re-negotiations for ever-increasing, ratchet-like expansion. Probably more than any other feature of the treaty, it is this unlimited commitment to ever-higher levels of liberalization that give rise to the greatest concern. Over the long term, a WTO services treaty with an ever-expanding reach poses a very grave threat indeed to public service systems throughout the world.

What are the chief concerns for the future of public education under an ever-expanding GATS?

4.2 Treaty by stealth? The problems of legal uncertainty and misunderstanding

Surprisingly few government representatives have demonstrated an adequate appreciation of the full sweep and the enormous implications of even the existing treaty. Such a lack of understanding is, to a considerable degree, understandable, given the treaty's maze-like complexity and expansive scope. However, there are also indications that proponents of the treaty have sometimes obfuscated the facts and have repeatedly made carefully crafted assertions that appear designed to mislead governments and the public[2].

For example, in response to growing public criticism, some prominent GATS proponents have sought to downplay the treaty's significance. They have pointed to non-binding language in the treaty's preamble, for example, that "recognizes the right of Members to regulate"— potentially leaving unwary readers with the impression that the treaty has little or no impact on member countries' regulatory ability. But the treaty is expressly designed to constrain —and clearly does constrain—governments' regulatory ability.

Officials have also made statements that leave the false impression that public services are fully shielded from the treaty's rules[3]—a regrettable stance that could be especially critical for the future of public education.

Basic misunderstandings about the GATS—whatever their cause—could have serious consequences, especially if, as now appears to be the case, mistaken impressions are widely held among those political representatives responsible for overseeing GATS negotiations.

There are at least three major dangers associated with such misunderstandings about the treaty.

Firstly, there is an increased risk of inadvertent coverage of public services. If ministers or negotiators believe—wrongly—that public services are fully excluded from the treaty, they may be willing to make new or more expansive specific commitments that will ultimately be found to have exposed important aspects of public service systems to GATS challenge.

Secondly, there is an increased potential for increased coverage of public services by stealth. For those governments or trade officials seeking to impose regulatory changes in public education or other sensitive areas, indirectly and secretly, or with "plausible deniability," the imposition becomes politically more feasible if government colleagues and citizens believe that GATS rules do not reach into the sensitive regulatory area in question.

Thirdly, there is an increased risk that the authority to clarify key aspects of the treaty will be determined solely by unelected WTO dispute panelists. By failing to clarify key aspects of the treaty, member governments are in effect ceding the authority for such clarification—even (or perhaps especially) in sensitive areas—to dispute panelists who often have little expertise in the policy area and who have no legitimate authority for balancing often-competing public policy priorities.

In light of these dangers, clarifying uncertainties in the existing treaty should be a key aspect of ongoing negotiations, and responsible governments should consider making such clarifications a precondition of further negotiations. Unfortunately, the main thrust of the WTO Secretariat, and of some key GATS proponents, is not to embark on this worthy task. Rather, the emphasis appears to be on belittling critics and their concerns while reiterating misleading assurances[4] as negotiators prepare to make new, more extensive commitments to extend the treaty's reach.

This approach, if it continues, greatly increases the likelihood that the treaty will affect public education systems even more seriously in future. Without firm action from governments to provide effective GATS safeguards, there is good reason to expect that the current round of negotiations will worsen the threats that the current treaty already poses for public education systems.

4.3 Unrelenting pressure for new, more extensive GATS specific commitments

At this stage of negotiations, it is not possible to determine what new commitments Canada or any other member country will be prepared to make in the current GATS negotiating round. Nor is it possible to know what commitments future governments may subsequently make. Thus, any discussion of specifics necessarily involves some degree of conjecture. It is clear, however, that governments face intense pressure to make new, more extensive specific commitments. For example, firms seeking expanded markets overseas can be expected to apply pressure on their governments to use the GATS process to gain market-opening concessions in other member countries.

Similarly, foreign firms apply pressure on *their* governments to extract equivalent concessions domestically. This effect exacerbates a common ideological bent of governments towards deregulation and a public policy atmosphere that is dominated by exhortations for greater 'trade' liberalization. Whatever the source of this pressure, it is strong and unrelenting.

In such a negotiating atmosphere, Canada, as one of the strongest proponents of GATS expansion, is likely to make substantial new GATS commitments. One of the simplest ways for a member to approach new GATS commitments is to offer market-opening commitments domestically in the same sector for which it seeks equivalent commitments from other members. Thus, for example, Canada could request other members to make specific commitments applying to curriculum development services, testing services, tutoring services, or specialist teaching services such as English as a second language (ESL) and speech therapy. Although reciprocity is not a requirement of the negotiating process, Canada could in turn offer corresponding liberalizing commitments, which would also enhance market access for service providers operating domestically.

The current federal government has repeatedly stated that it will not make GATS commitments covering "public education." This statement leaves the door open to commitments covering "private education." Any commitments covering private education would have important legal implications for the public system. But, even if the Canadian government makes no commitments covering education in the current round, it is important to examine the policy implications of greater GATS coverage that could occur in future rounds.

Any future federal government may decide to make commitments, whether in response to pressure from the corporate sector, foreign governments, or of its own ideological volition. Once made, such commitments will be very difficult for succeeding governments to undo. Furthermore, as more and more sectors are committed, the rising tide increases pressure to cover those sensitive sectors, such as education, that remain relatively uncommitted. Finally, given the treaty's inherent bias towards expansion, it is sensible to assume that some day the GATS rules will apply more fully to the education sector. The legitimacy of the GATS as a multilateral framework for regulating services should be judged accordingly.

If Canada makes broader commitments on a range of education services, this would entail greater risks for Canadian public education systems, as the following hypothetical examples suggest.

4.3.1 National treatment

The ability of foreign education service providers to extract public subsidies from Canadian governments is likely to be particularly contentious in future. In particular, foreign for-profit providers are likely to seek subsidies that are equivalent not simply to those provided to their private counterparts in Canada, but to the higher subsidies provided to public schools.

Hypothetical example
Expanding Canada's national treatment obligations: opening a Pandora's box of subsidies issues?
Canada, acting on the false premise that public services are beyond the reach of GATS rules, commits to applying the national treatment rule to all subsidies provided in Canada

to private, for-profit schools. When criticized for the initiative, the federal trade minister stresses that the commitment merely provides private for-profit education providers from other countries access to the same subsidies that are given to private for-profit education providers based in Canada. He emphasizes that the commitment does not extend to subsidies provided to *public* education and that *public* education is therefore not at risk.

On behalf of a newly-formed coalition of education management organizations (EMOs)[5] operating in Canada, the U.S. government mounts a GATS challenge, demanding for these companies subsidies equivalent to Canadian *public* (not just private) schools. In the ensuing case, the U.S. argues that American EMOs provide a "like" service to those provided by the Canadian public schools, and that Canadian public school boards "compete" with their private counterparts and therefore do not fall within the protective governmental authority exclusion.[6]

Critically, the U.S. also challenges the meaning of Canada's horizontal limitation on national treatment, listed in its schedule of commitments since 1994, asserting that it does not protect new GATS-inconsistent measures. National treatment rules therefore apply, the U.S. argues, and Canada must grant U.S.-based EMOs subsidies equivalent to those offered their Canadian counterparts.

Finally, the U.S. argues that, even if this interpretation is rejected, Canada must supply equivalent subsidies to private suppliers anyway, because not to do so would violate the treaty's market access rules,[7] against which Canada listed no protective limitation.

Is there any basis for these disturbing hypothetical claims? Or does a key clause, contained in Canada's schedule of commitments, fully protect against such challenges?

To answer these questions, it is necessary to examine one of the most important "horizontal commitments" that Canada made when it adopted the GATS in 1994. In its schedule of specific commitments, Canada registered the following limitation on national treatment:

"*The supply of a service, or its subsidization, within the public sector is not in breach of this commitment.*"

Will this key clause actually protect against the types of challenges considered in the above example? Unfortunately, the provision raises more issues than it resolves:

- Does Canada's horizontal limitation on national treatment reinforce concerns about the perceived adequacy of the GATS governmental authority exclusion? If, as proponents claim, public services are already fully protected by the general exclusion,[8] what is the purpose of this limitation?
- Is Canada's limitation broad or narrow? What is the precise meaning of the phrase "within the public sector"? How would GATS dispute panels interpret it?
- Why is Canada's provision "bound"? Does this mean that it protects only *existing* non-conforming measures? Does it fail to protect future measures—for example, a future provincial government restriction on new or increased subsidies to public, not-for-profit service providers?
- Why is Canada's limitation so different from the equivalent U.S. version?[9] Why did Canada not employ the same strategy—making "unbound" limitations for subsidies in both the national treatment and market access categories, thereby providing far more definitive protection?

Perilous Lessons 113

- Why is Canada's limitation for public service subsidies so different from the limitation for research and development subsidies, which is "unbound"?[10]
- Why is Canada's limitation for public service subsidies that is listed under national treatment not matched by an equivalent limitation under market access? This seems especially important in light of the fact that differential subsidization based on the "specific type of legal entity" is likely to be found to violate not just national treatment rules, but market access rules as well[11]. In other words, did Canada ensure its continued ability to provide differential subsidization by allowing it to escape the national treatment "trap" by means of this limitation, only to be caught anyway by the GATS market access provision, against which Canada failed to provide equivalent protection?

Whatever the answers to these questions, one thing is clear. *In its horizontal, 'across-the-board' GATS commitments, Canada appears to have failed to protect, unequivocally, its ability to withhold public subsidies from foreign service suppliers if such subsidies are granted to Canadian suppliers, whether public or private.* As a result, for every service Canada agrees to make subject to the GATS national treatment rule, non-discriminatory subsidization may be required unless a limitation allowing for differential subsidization is specifically listed for every committed service.[12]

4.3.2 Market access

As previously discussed, the GATS market access rules are novel and onerous. Like the national treatment rules, these provisions do not now apply to education services, as Canada has not made specific commitments in this sector. However, market access commitments in education services could have similarly complex and serious ramifications for public education systems in ways that are difficult to predict.

Hypothetical example
Expanding market access commitments: another Pandora's box
Seeking greater market access overseas for its education service providers, Canada requests other countries to make market access commitments in education. In response to reciprocal requests, Canada also makes specific commitments in education services, but limits its GATS commitments in market access to "commercial education services."

In partnership with its new Canadian affiliate, a U.S.-based commercial education provider enters the Canadian market, contracting with private school boards in several provinces to manage certain of their schools. Facing a flat market in difficult economic times, the company seeks to expand into more lucrative markets, offering to provide public school boards such services as school evaluation,[13] testing students' academic achievement, recruiting teachers, administrators and other staff, providing school secretarial services and cleaning services for school buildings and administrative offices. Through a subsidiary, it also applies to several provinces for the right to establish, manage and operate its own school districts and to receive public funding equivalent to that provided to public school boards.

In an ensuing GATS dispute, the United States argues that Canada's limitation on market access to "commercial education services" does not apply to school evaluation services, student testing, recruitment of staff, the provision of secretarial or cleaning services. These services, it notes, are classified in the GATS as *Business Services* (CPC 87[14]) for which Canada has previously made unlimited specific commitments. As for the establishment, management and operation of school districts, the U.S. argues that these services are performed for a specified fee and so are commercial in nature, and so are covered by Canada's specific commitment.

Moreover, according to the U.S., the failure on the part of Canada (or any of its provinces or "regional subdivisions") to permit new school boards amounts to a "limitation on the number of service suppliers," as well as a measure that "requires specific types of legal entity," which are expressly prohibited by GATS Article XVI(2)(a) and (e). Finally, the U.S. argues that the failure by Canadian provinces to provide the company public funding amounts to an abuse of existing school boards' monopoly rights, prohibited by Article VIII(1), which specifies that activities of monopolies and exclusive service suppliers must be consistent with a Member's specific commitments—in this case, market access and national treatment.

4.3.3 Classification issues

It is relatively easy to see how differences concerning the classification of services can lead to disputes about the coverage of particular services and the application of particular GATS obligations. It is also easy to see how such services as school evaluation services, testing services, library services, curriculum development services, secretarial services, specialist teaching services, tutoring services, food services, cleaning services, and counselling services could be carved away from what is now considered the public education system—and directly subjected to GATS rules and dispute settlement.[15]

What is not so immediately obvious is that even GATS disputes involving services that may not generally be considered *Education Services* also have the potential to affect fundamental aspects of Canada's public education systems. Even the basic issue of public funding could emerge as a result of a dispute involving the coverage, or exclusion, of particular services and the application to that service of a particular GATS obligation.

Hypothetical example
Making new commitments—even in services that are not obviously education-related—could facilitate the entry of U.S. EMOs
At the request of the United States, Canada agrees to make unlimited market access commitments in a range of *Business Services* (classified in CPC Section 8). A private U.S.-based education service provider with strong political connections to the U.S. government, anxious to expand into Canada, demands the right to manage and operate schools in Canada. Arguing its case before a WTO dispute settlement panel, the U.S. government asserts that, with the possible exception of classroom teaching, most of the services involved in managing and operating schools are not in fact *Education Services*. Rather, many are *Business Services* and, as a result, the U.S. asserts, are fully subject to the unlimited market access commitments made by Canada.

Classification issues involving education are likely to become increasingly contentious. In a paper released in May 2002, the Liberalization of Trade in Services Committee of the International Financial Services Organization of London[16] explicitly distinguishes between "core" and "ancillary" education services, arguing for increased liberalization of the latter within the GATS.[17]

No one knows which types of issues, if any, highlighted in the above examples could result in actual GATS disputes. After all, it is not possible to know the outcome of negotiations that are still under way or future negotiations that have not yet begun. If the Canadian government were to make additional specific commitments in this round, past practice suggests that Canadian citizens will learn of those commitments only after they have been formally presented to other countries in Geneva.

The purpose of considering such examples, therefore, is not to predict the course of future negotiations, but to illustrate the complexities and range of risks involved in making new specific commitments. In principle, Canada has the ability, in this round, to avoid the pitfalls the examples highlight. Unfortunately, in the absence of significant changes to the substance of the treaty, this alone is not sufficient. To fully safeguard the country's public education system from GATS rules, Canada must avoid *every one* of these pitfalls, and others that are not been discussed here or that have yet to be identified—and then not just during this round but, without exception, *in all subsequent negotiating rounds*. The prospects that this high standard of vigilance can be sustained indefinitely seem remote.

4.4. Pressure for other GATS concessions

The pressure that results from negotiations to continually expand the GATS is not limited to pressure on members to expand their specific commitments. Members also face demands to extend obligations contained in other provisions in the treaty. This pressure is likely to be at least as intense, and its results could prove just as significant for public education systems. Such pressure amounts to an unending war of attrition on all measures that are contrary to ever-tightening GATS rules.

In practical terms, this type of negotiation transfers the onus of justifying change away from GATS proponents, as ever-increasing market access for commercial education is widely perceived to be the new status quo. Instead, the onus is shifted to governments that seek to defend their regulatory authority, in effect requiring them as never before to justify measures that may conflict with the principles of a binding treaty they have already adopted. The pressure also forces sub-national governments and public education advocates further to the margins, even though these governments may have direct responsibility for education policy and even though, unlike federal trade negotiators, they often have an intimate working knowledge of the issues at stake in the relevant sectors.

4.4.1 GATS negotiations on Domestic Regulation

Of all the areas where Canada could make concessions, other than in making additional specific commitments, the negotiations on domestic regulation are of greatest concern. As noted in Section 2.3.3, members have agreed to develop new constraints on non-discriminatory regulatory measures taken by governments. It is important to recognize that these proposed rules have a number of features that would give them extraordinary power.[18]

Firstly, the proposed rules are designed to act like a new fine-meshed drift net—capturing government measures that would bypass all of the other GATS constraints. Thus, even government measures that are consistent with the tough non-discrimination rules contained in the GATS MFN and national treatment articles, and even those that are consistent with the GATS market access provisions, could be found to violate the proposed domestic regulation restrictions.

Secondly, these proposed rules would cover subject matter that is very broad and highly relevant to education. They extend to "measures *relating* to qualification requirements and procedures, technical standards and licensing procedures"[19]. While these terms are not defined precisely in the treaty, they can be expected to include, for example, professional accreditation, certification of schools, certification of school boards, and the licensing of school facilities. Indeed, the list of affected measures in the education sector is likely to be very long since, for example, even the term "technical standards" is likely to be interpreted broadly. According to the WTO Secretariat, it refers not just to the "technical characteristics of the service itself" but also to "the rules according to which the service must be performed."[20]

Thirdly, the proposed restrictions are intended to apply a test of "necessity" to measures covered by this broad provision. That is, governments would face the difficult onus of demonstrating that their regulations affecting the public education system were "necessary" to achieve a legitimate objective. Governments would also have to prove that no alternative measure was available that was less commercially restrictive. While the precise application of these concepts is now under negotiation, there can be little doubt that the intent is for their application to capture a very wide range of government regulations.[21]

Fourthly, though it is a matter for negotiation, it is possible that the proposed GATS domestic regulation rules will apply across-the-board to all measures, even to those for which members have made no specific commitments.[22]

Finally, whatever domestic regulation rules are agreed to during negotiations, they are likely to apply without exception, since the article does not allow for any country-specific exceptions or limitations.[23] While the rules will not themselves establish global standards, they would ensure that domestic education standards and practices meet GATS rules—without exception.

Together, these features indicate that the GATS domestic regulation negotiations could soon bring public education systems even further within the purview of the WTO. If the negotiations proceed as expected, the resulting rules would allow dispute panels to oversee an extraordinarily broad range of domestic procedures and standards to ensure they meet GATS rules. These panels could second-guess policies concerning: commercial advertising in or around schools, student testing, the distribution of education materials, and licensing procedures for teachers and schools, especially where education-related services are contracted to commercial enterprises.[24]

In short, these panelists could be called upon to rule on aspects of those issues that are considered in the above hypothetical examples—and many more. The domestic regulation negotiations by themselves thus pose a profound threat to public education systems.

Chapter 5
Canada's approach in the current GATS round

As international trade and investment treaties stray further afield from tariffs and border matters, their negotiation involves increasingly complex and sensitive regulatory issues. The GATS is no exception. Its reach is so extraordinarily broad that it has the potential, as we have seen, to affect domestic education policy-making in diverse and unanticipated ways that are of profound significance to citizens.

In light of the numerous risks—both in the existing treaty and in repeated rounds of re-negotiations—the effective protection of public education and other public service systems requires governments to be sensitive to their citizens' priorities. It also demands that governments be unwaveringly committed to the sector's protection, studiously alert to the treaty's many risks, forthright with their citizens, and astute and sophisticated in their strategy.

Unfortunately, there are grounds for concern that these essential characteristics are exhibited far too rarely in the Canadian government's approach to GATS negotiations. Indeed, whether blithely, or knowingly and recklessly, *Canada seems to be taking an approach to GATS negotiations that could increase threats that the treaty already poses to Canada's K-12 public education system.*

5.1 Canada's stated GATS objectives for education: Unsustainable balancing act between conflicting aims?

Canada's approach to education in the current GATS negotiations is driven by two distinct and ultimately conflicting objectives.

On the one hand, Canada is seeking to expand exports of education-related services provided by Canadian service suppliers. The Department of Foreign Affairs and International Trade (DFAIT) is enthusiastic in its description of what it calls the "knowledge industry" and the prospects for exports in this sector:

"There has never been a better time for Canadians to export education and training products and services. As the world shifts from resource-based to knowledge-based economies, the demand for education and training services and products is increasing rapidly in all parts of the globe."[1]

DFAIT maintains an on-line resource centre "to assist the Canadian knowledge industry to promote and export its products and services effectively in international markets."[2]

While Canada's initial negotiating proposals in the current round of GATS negotiations do not specifically mention education services, Canada does note, as the first item on its list of objectives, that it aims "[t]o obtain improved access to international markets for Canadian service providers."[3] More specifically, the federal government indicates that it is "interested in promoting the export of Canadian educational services" through GATS negotiations.[4] The government also claims to have consulted widely on education in preparation for the GATS round, based on an extensive discussion paper on the sector prepared especially for the current negotiations.[5]

On the other hand, Canada professes to be intent on shielding public education within Canada from GATS rules. As the government's website states:
"Canada...has clearly stated that it will not negotiate its health, public education or social services, and that it will maintain its flexibility to pursue its cultural policy objectives."[6]

Canadian trade minister Pierre Pettigrew, using rather more colourful language in response to provincial concerns, asserted:
"I can tell you loud and clear that any suggestion that health and social services are in danger is preposterous."[7]

These two objectives—increasing education services exports from Canada while shielding Canadian education from GATS rules—are *technically* not in direct conflict. It is this understanding that underpins the Canadian negotiating position:
"The door will remain open for Canadian business and institutions to sell [educational services] abroad, even while Canada preserves its ability to maintain or establish regulations, subsidies, administrative practices or other measures in sectors such as health, public education and social services."[8]

Unfortunately, in practice, such technical distinctions are unlikely to carry much weight. As negotiations proceed, Canada's objectives for education are almost certain to be perceived, by foreign and Canadian negotiators alike, as in direct conflict.

Canada's GATS position on education certainly appears to be unsustainable. How long can Canada demand that other countries open up *their* critical education sectors while fully protecting its own, before the position is labelled hypocritical? At the very least, attempting to extract liberalization commitments from foreign governments would increase pressure on Canadian governments to make similar commitments—pressure that requires the spending of other negotiating coin, in other important sectors, to resist.

Setting aside the problem of the conflicting nature of its two objectives, Canada appears to have a preponderant focus on just one of the aims, at the expense of the other. Its principal aim appears to be on gaining greater market access in other countries for Canadian-based businesses. The federal government itself emphasizes this primary focus on its Services 2000 website:

> "Canada's overall objective in the GATS negotiations is to improve the well-being of Canadians by securing access to foreign markets for our service providers and by establishing a rules-based trading system that will protect Canadian business from unfair competition or discrimination."[9]

This objective, which is reflected in much of the government's published material and in its consultation process, is unlikely to provoke controversy. However, the basis for such a focus in the education sector remains unclear. And what is controversial, of course, is the extent to which this stress on export development eclipses safeguarding and enhancing Canada's public service systems.

What is the basis for this export development focus in the GATS? Clearly, a growing number of Canadian firms and institutions export education services. But the volumes of this trade are very low. A recent report prepared for the federal government[10] indicates that services in general are "less traded than most goods". Indeed, "the socially sensitive sectors of education and health...[have] miniscule trade exposure."[11] According to this report, the dependence on trade—that is, the ratio of domestic exports to GDP—for education is only 1.4%. This includes transactions associated with students studying abroad and, while greater than for health and social services (0.4%), is far less than the trade dependence for business services (23.4%), insurance (27.0%), and professional services (38.4%), and markedly less than for all services (11.8%).[12]

Even for those firms that do export, the potential economic benefit of further liberalization has not been rigorously assessed.[13] More particularly, Canadian trade officials themselves admit that Canadian education service providers operating overseas currently face few trade barriers[14]. Further liberalization could thus be expected to provide these providers, at best, with only modest benefits.[15] Despite this, counting on GATS to deliver benefits for Canadian companies appears to be almost an article of faith, and the export development priority dominates Canada's position.

By contrast, Canadian government consultations have identified widespread public concerns about the risks GATS negotiations pose to Canada's public education system.[16] Perhaps Canadian representatives are convinced that Canada can eliminate the GATS threats to its public education system entirely. Or perhaps officials believe that these threats are outweighed by the potential benefits to

Canadian companies operating overseas. In any event, the available evidence supports neither of these propositions, and the predominant emphasis placed on increasing Canadian education services exports remains as puzzling as it is ominous.

5.2 Poised to make specific commitments affecting education

The Canadian government appears poised to make GATS specific commitments that could affect the country's public education system. As a result, the government's confidence in its ability to protect public education systems against the force of GATS rules may soon be tested.

The government is apparently prepared to make GATS-specific commitments in services that are provided as part of Canada's public education system, but which may formally be classified within a different sector. For example, in a series of questions and answers prepared for the federal trade minister, officials recently emphasized the limits to the education service category, stating in one of their answers: "Let's keep clear that janitorial or food services are just that: they are not educational services when provided in schools."[17]

This same logic, of course, could be applied to many other services, suggesting that the government may be prepared to make specific commitments in a range of sectors within the public education sphere, while retaining its ability to claim that it is making no commitments in education services, per se. Such a strategy has the effect of chipping away, or diminishing, the number and types of services within the public education system that are excluded from GATS rules.

Even more significantly, the government appears to be prepared to make GATS-specific commitments in areas that unequivocally and indisputably are classified as education services under the treaty. In particular, the government is poised to make specific commitments in so-called 'commercial' education. The government's own GATS discussion paper explicitly contemplates this, asking: "Should Commercial Education and Training Services be Included in Canada's Trade Commitments?"[18] Moreover, Trade Minister Pierre Pettigrew strongly suggests that this possibility is under active consideration, stating:

> "[T]he Government of Canada will not undertake any commitments in the public education sector...Regarding commercial education and training services, the Canadian position is still being developed...I can assure you that any approach taken by Canada on commercial education and training services will not impede Canada's ability to regulate and protect our public education."[19]

In addition, there are many pieces of indirect evidence that are consistent with such an approach and, when considered together, strongly suggest—at a minimum—that Canada has not ruled out making specific commitments in "commercial" education.

Government representatives have made numerous statements that are meant to reassure the public about the potential impact of GATS negotiations on education. With very few exceptions, these statements draw a distinction between public and other types of education, and generally avoid clear commitments to protect, for example, *education* from the application of GATS rules, or to protect *Canada's education sector*, or education services. Time and again, government representatives restrict their comments to protecting *public* education, suggesting that the government is prepared to make commitments in aspects of the education system they do not deem to be *public*.

For example, as noted above, Minister Pettigrew has asserted that "the Government of Canada will not undertake any commitments in the *public* education sector."[20] He has also stated that "Canadian authorities at all levels maintain the right to regulate the *public* education system."[21] Government officials have also asserted that, as a "bottom line", "*Public* education is not negotiable"[22] and that "Canada's ability to adopt or maintain ...measures in *public* education is preserved".[23]

Officials also edited material for the government's website dealing with protection afforded to education under the GATS, specifically changing "*education*" to "*public education*."[24] The resulting text reasserts that "Canada will preserve its ability to maintain or establish regulations, subsidies, administrative practices or other measures in sectors such as...*public education*."[25]

Taken together, these statements support the contention that *Canada appears to be prepared to make specific commitments in some education services in the current round of GATS negotiations*. Though it has often been asserted that Canada's position has not yet been finalized, that such specific commitments apparently are under active consideration has never, to the authors' knowledge, been denied. Instead, the government's focus has been on providing statements designed to reassure the public about GATS issues that could arise. The vital question of what, according to the Canadian government, constitutes *public education*—as opposed to *commercial education* or any other type of education—is seldom, if ever, openly acknowledged or publicly discussed. This points toward the startling conclusion that federal representatives may themselves be either unclear on, or unconcerned about, precisely what aspects of this vital sector are to be subjected to the most onerous GATS rules—even as sensitive negotiations are well under way.[26]

5.3 Playing down the risks: Providing unbalanced, misleading information to the public

That Canadian government representatives do not seem clear on what aspects of Canada's education system should be subjected to WTO oversight is worrisome in itself. But this concern is augmented by a perception that negotiators have not demonstrated, or do not have, an adequate appreciation of public education and the GATS negotiation process. For example, while government representatives frequently extol the virtues of increasing market access overseas, they seldom demonstrate equivalent enthusiasm for maintaining—fully intact—Canada's existing public education system.[27]

More specifically, there is also little or no public recognition of the 'ratchet effect' of GATS negotiations, where failed experiments in liberalization are all but irreversible in practice. And there is little if any public acknowledgement of the fact that intense pressure will be brought to bear on Canada's education system, not just during the current round of GATS negotiations, but during repeated re-negotiations over the long term. In short, government representatives consistently understate the importance and the degree to which GATS does now, and could in future, diminish governments' regulatory authority in Canada's public education system.

But this lack of balance seems minor compared with government statements about public education that are designed to be reassuring but which are distressingly misleading.

Some of statements appear to be satisfyingly comprehensive and clear. For example, Industry Canada's GATS negotiations website states categorically that "[t]he health and public education systems that Canadians cherish will not be put at risk in the GATS negotiations."[28] Also, in response to the question: "Is Canada's public education system threatened?", it offers a flat "No," adding: "Our public education system is not negotiable."[29]

Such comprehensive statements are welcome. But they demand close scrutiny. In the context of GATS negotiations, their substance hinges on the definition given to public education. Do the statements reflect a genuine commitment on the part of the government to fully protect Canada's public education system, broadly defined? Alternatively, are these statements highly misleading, utilizing an unusual and very narrow definition of *public education*? So long as the government's definition remains unclear, the meaning of these statements—reassuring though they may sound—remains shrouded in ambiguity.

Unfortunately, many other government statements are even more ambiguous; others are confused or misleading. These statements, including those considered below, raise further concerns about Canada's negotiating position.

5.3.1 Assertion: Governments' regulatory ability is protected

It is frequently asserted, for example, that, despite GATS negotiations, Canada will maintain its regulatory ability. As previously noted, Trade Minister Pettigrew has asserted that "Canadian authorities at all levels maintain the right to regulate the public education system, based on Canadian objectives and priorities."[30] The public record contains many reiterations of this theme. It should be noted that the Minister does not state that the public education system is unaffected by the GATS. Neither does he assert that governments' right to regulate that system is undiminished by the GATS. The stated claim is in fact far narrower: merely that governments retain the "right to regulate"...and then, "based on Canadian objectives and priorities".[31] What the Minister does not state is that this right to regulate is subject to GATS constraints; that is, all resulting government measures must conform to applicable GATS rules.

5.3.2 Assertion: Canada retains the right to maintain public services

As noted above[32], Canada asserted, when it submitted its GATS commitments in 1994, that "[t]he supply of a service... within the public sector is not in breach" of the GATS national treatment obligation. In March 2001, in its formal negotiating proposal submitted to the WTO, Canada asserts:

> "We recognize the right of individual countries to maintain public services in sectors of their choice. This is not a matter for the GATS negotiations."[33]

These statements, particularly the more recent, which focuses narrowly on the maintenance of public services, are far from reassuring. They appear to call into question governments' ability to establish new public services and their ability—unfettered by GATS rules—to regulate mixed public service systems.[34]

5.3.3 Assertion: Public education is not negotiable

As noted above in a different context, Canada's Services 2000 website categorically states that "Our public education system is not negotiable."[35] This claim has also been made by government officials in presentations across the country.[36] And in Oral Question Period in the House of Commons, Trade Minister Pettigrew stated that:

> "I have been as clear as I can possibly be that the government will not negotiate our health system or our public education system."[37]

Unfortunately, aspects of public education systems are *already* under negotiation in Geneva, whether the Canadian government or citizens like it or not. Negotiating proposals by the United States, New Zealand, and especially the more recent GATS proposals by Australia,[38] clearly touch on matters of direct relevance to public education systems. While it may make no specific commitments or other GATS concessions in the education sector, to suggest that public education is not negotiable—in the sense that public education services are not and will not be negotiated[39] —is simply untenable.[40] Indeed, federal officials occasionally acknowledge this fact themselves. Material for presentation to the Council of Ministers of Education and to the Canadian Teachers' Federation state:

> "Notwithstanding our position on public education, we must anticipate a requirement to discuss with WTO members proposals that relate to education."[41]

Not only are important aspects of public education systems negotiable, they are currently <u>being</u> negotiated at meetings, in which Canadian officials attend and participate, in Geneva.

5.3.4 Assertion: GATS does not require privatization or deregulation

The Canadian government, like the WTO Secretariat, frequently claims that the GATS does not require public service systems to be privatized or deregulated.[42] While technically true, as has been emphasized elsewhere,[43] this assertion is very misleading. Governments will remain subject to constant pressure, through repeated GATS renegotiations, to open public service systems to foreign commercial providers. It is also a disservice to neglect to note that GATS provisions help consolidate commercialization wherever it occurs.[44]

5.3.5 Assertion: Canada's public education is protected: Revisiting the 'governmental authority' exclusion

> "Mr. Speaker, the GATS explicitly excludes 'services supplied in the exercise of governmental authority.' With respect to these services, it is absolutely clear."
> —Hon. Pierre Pettigrew, Minister for International Trade
> Oral Question Period, House of Commons, February 19, 2001.[45]

Of all the questionable assertions made by federal government representatives about the GATS and public education, the claim that public education is protected by the 'governmental authority' exclusion is perhaps the most troubling. The significance of this exclusion has already been considered.[46] As we have seen, the exclusion is unlikely to protect many aspects of Canada's public education system from GATS rules, as the exclusion is very narrow and is likely to be interpreted restrictively. It is particularly disturbing, therefore, to note that the federal government continues to assert that Canada's public education system is protected largely through the existence of this narrow exclusion.[47]

What is even more troubling, however, is that there does not appear to be a clear and consistent understanding—within the federal government—of Canada's own interpretation of the exclusion.

For example, even the government's discussion paper, "The Commercial Education and Training Services Industry,"[48] prepared specifically for GATS negotiations, employs several different interpretations of the exclusion. It states, for example, that "basic education *provided by the State*...is considered to fall within the domain of services supplied in the exercise of governmental authority...."[49] By contrast, the same document states elsewhere that "Basic education...is often provided by (*or with support from*) public authorities...[and] [s]uch education services...are considered services 'supplied in the exercise of governmental authority' and thus...not covered by the GATS."[50]

On another page, the same document asserts[51] that, "[s]ince many educational services in Canada are provided by or with the support of the government, this sector was viewed as being outside the competitive domain." While this reference implies that such services are thereby excluded from the GATS, it does not specifically say so. And the observation that the reference appears to ignore the second essential criteria for any service to be excluded—namely, that it is provided on a non-commercial basis—may be splitting hairs.

What is most disconcerting about this reference is that it suggests that, since "many educational services" are provided by or with the support of the government, the entire educational service sector is viewed as being non-competitive. Surely, one must object, these concerns are merely errors in drafting—and they probably are. But they are likely made by the very officials who would be primarily responsible, under intense pressure, for crafting Canada's negotiating text on education services.

Finally, the education discussion paper states: "[t]he GATS covers only primary, secondary, tertiary/higher, adult, and other educational services supplied on a commercial basis where competition is allowed." Here it is noteworthy that, through its omission of one critical word—"or"—the document misrepresents the meaning of the relevant GATS text. Services are covered whenever they are provided on a commercial basis or where competition occurs.[52]

Unfortunately, whether through inattention to detail, lack of adequate understanding, or some other reason, other government pronouncements are at least as problematic. Some are profoundly troubling. For example, material prepared by federal officials for their presentations to provincial education ministers in April 2001 states:

"Article 1(3)(c) [the governmental authority exclusion] is meant to cover...services made available to the public on a universal basis, such as...public education."

This is a bald assertion that is clearly unsupported by, and indeed conflicts with, the GATS text.[53] A similar formulation appeared in internal government documents two years earlier, suggesting that its substance may be widely, and inappropriately, taken as fact: *"The GATS does not cover ...services supplied in the exercise of governmental authority, such as public education."* (emphasis in original).[54]

What is distressing about the above references is not that some of them are less than precise or that officials got a word wrong here or there. Naturally, the existence of so many inconsistent interpretations that are widely disseminated within the federal government is itself a matter of some concern. But what is so utterly shocking is that, *whatever their source*—whether from the government's own discussion paper, internal documents, or briefing material for presentation to provincial ministers—*every one of the references cited above are either misleading, at odds with the ordinary meaning of the GATS text, or both.* This alarming degree of imprecision or outright shiftiness about fundamental issues raises serious concerns about the impacts Canada's GATS negotiating approach could have on the country's public education system.

Chapter 6
Revising the lesson: conclusion and recommendations

There was a time when public education advocates didn't need to pay much attention to international "trade" treaties. Those days are gone.

As this report demonstrates, the GATS—and negotiations to expand the treaty—pose a real and present danger to Canada's public education system. Fortunately, Canada retains a significant degree of policy flexibility in the sector, and a variety of practical means exist to reduce many of these risks, and even to eliminate some of them.

More fundamentally, citizens have demonstrated their ability, when acting together, to play a key role in addressing some of the underlying conflicts between the country's international trade policy and its citizens' priorities. The task at hand is to begin to bring that powerful influence to bear to protect and enhance Canada's public education system.

6.1 GATS: Casting a lengthening shadow over education

Inevitably, the GATS comes across as an impenetrable treaty remote from the concerns of parents who entrust their children's education to our public schools, and from the daily challenges of teachers and other people who make our schools work. And that's the mistaken impression our federal government would probably like to perpetuate as it prepares to negotiate GATS rules affecting education services.

In fact, the GATS already casts a shadow over Canada's public education system.

Many common activities within our public school systems have already entered the vast orbit of international trade in services, as defined by the treaty. Initiatives that take place entirely within Canada for entirely educational purposes can nevertheless be defined as international trade relationships. Understanding how this is so requires following the Alice-in-Wonderland logic of the GATS, in which trade in services is defined to be nearly all-encompassing:

- Teachers promote trade in an educational service when they advise worried parents to prepare their children for new province-wide tests by enrolling their children in the local franchise of a foreign-owned tutoring agency.
- Educators may be competing with international suppliers when they design an Internet-based course to expand access to public education in remote locations.
- Local school boards compete with other public and private institutions when they recruit international fee-paying students.
- School boards become suppliers of a commercial business service, competing against other domestic and international suppliers, when they sell advertising space on their buses and school properties.
- Education administrators enter into an international investment arrangement when they seek private financing for new school construction.

In each of these cases, under the existing GATS or under an expanded treaty, GATS restrictions do, or soon could, apply.

With increasing commercialization, the number of "trade relationships" in which schools participate will multiply. Indeed, the entire operations of public schools—including classroom instruction, administration, and all support services—could become potentially traded services, subject to GATS scrutiny, if foreign-based education management organizations, of the type described in Chapter 3 of this report, are allowed to proliferate in Canada.

While the GATS rules apply unevenly, the sweeping scope of the agreement already requires that astute policy-makers and educational authorities consider the trade policy implications of their decisions. A trade screen for education policy must at a minimum consider the GATS rules that now apply to all services:

- **Most-Favoured Nation rule:** Does one provincially-funded contract with an American educational testing corporation require school boards throughout the province to provide the same level of access to public funding for all foreign –based providers of the same service?
- **Transparency rule:** Are local authorities setting up GATS-inconsistent trade barriers when they prevent schools from selling advertising space or granting franchises to soft-drink vendors, and must other WTO members be notified of these so-called "trade barriers"?

Other GATS general rules affecting the public education system are triggered if a government makes specific commitments covering commercial education:

- **Constraints on domestic regulation:** Could curriculum guidelines which require inclusion of locally-specific content, such as the history of Aboriginal peoples in the area, be challenged as more trade-restric-

tive than necessary to achieve their educational objective?
- **Monopoly rules:** Could a provincial education ministry that develops curriculum for the Internet be challenged as abusing its monopoly position if it does not recognize privately-offered distance-education courses as having equivalent credit towards completion of a high-school diploma?

WTO trade tribunals have shown a strong predilection, even determination, to interpret GATS rules expansively. Whether GATS rules would be seen to apply or be enforced in the above examples would depend on the particular circumstances of the trade dispute and the make-up of the WTO dispute settlement panel. Not only would such a WTO panel be unaccountable to local citizenry, but in all likelihood it would also be unfamiliar and unconcerned with the complex financial and regulatory framework in which Canadian educational policy is applied.

Even the possibility of exposure to these rules casts a pall over education policy as policy-makers understandably shy away from innovative practices that are so necessary for strengthening our education system on the basis that they may also be GATS-inconsistent.

This pall would only be exacerbated if Canada negotiates commitments making "commercial education and training" subject to the most forceful GATS rules. This category of education services, which is nowhere defined in the GATS, is not easily delineated in public school systems that increasingly rely on private sources of financing and commercially-provided services, and which increasingly compete with private education providers.

Changes in obscure classification systems could determine whether or not a particular activity is subject to the full force of the GATS. Were Canada to make such a commitment, how would teachers, administrators and elected officials know at what point they are entering into a commercial education service, and are expected by the federal government, therefore, to comply with the stringent GATS national treatment and market access rules?

The chill could be further worsened by a GATS negotiating agenda that includes formulating new, untested rules. These rules could apply universally in all service sectors or selectively in specific service sectors committed by Canada.

- Will policy-makers soon have to take into account new rules on subsidies, which could strengthen private school claims for increased levels of public funding?
- Will new rules on government procurement require all contracts of significant size to be tendered internationally?
- Will new rules on domestic regulation force education to continually demonstrate that they have opted for the least trade-restrictive requirements and practices for granting licenses, for establishing qualifications, and for setting educational standards?

6.2 Reassurances from the federal government: overly optimistic and misleading

Canadian government representatives maintain that none of these concerns is valid. There are no significant implications for our K-12 education systems, they say, because Canada has made no education commitments in the GATS and will not negotiate public education commitments in the current and future services negotiations. Furthermore, they add, an exclusion for public services ensures that the GATS does not apply to public schools.

As our study shows, these reassurances are misleading. Within the International Trade Minister's apparently categorical commitments in Parliament are very carefully constructed phrases that gloss over the government's preparations to negotiate away certain aspects of our education systems. Documents obtained through Access to Information trace a very deliberate revision of the government's public position. The government has affirmed its intention to refrain only from making specific commitments in *public education;* this leaves it the option to make commitments in the broader category of *education.*

At the same time, in more candid settings, government officials acknowledge the conceptual difficulty in clearly distinguishing between *commercial education and training* and *public education.* Government reassurances presume a clear demarcation between commercial and public services within our public school systems—a demarcation that does not in fact exist. These reassurances also defy the GATS classification for education services, which does not distinguish between commercial and publicly-provided education.

Our close examination of the "governmental authority" exclusion shows not only that federal government assertions regarding its significance are exaggerated, but also that inconsistent and incorrect interpretations are repeatedly made by and within the federal government. Given the enormous and, in our view, unwarranted faith our government puts in the ability of this exclusion to safeguard education and other public services, and the confident position conveyed to Canadians, it is very troubling to discover confusion within the federal government about what this crucial provision really means. It is even more distressing to learn that the federal government's description of the critical exemption, contained in official public documents, conflicts with an ordinary reading of the treaty text.

6.3 Changing Canada's approach to the GATS and education

So what does all this mean for Canadians committed to maintaining, and enhancing, a vibrant public education system?

The principles of the GATS are, at root, in conflict with those of Canada's public education system. The impetus of the GATS is to expand commercial opportunities for foreign service providers and investors—in short, to commercialize services. Canada's public education system exists to ensure free, high-quality education for all regardless of their financial circumstances or ability to pay. As the ever-expanding treaty envisioned in current GATS negotiations encroaches on public service sectors that have been deliberately shielded from market imperatives, public education would become distorted and constricted, a situation that is grim, unsatisfactory and unacceptable. A radical shift in Canada's approach to education in the GATS—and to the GATS itself—is urgently required.

The good news is that such a shift in trade policy is feasible; Canadians can still ensure that the most restrictive GATS rules do not apply to most education services, and need not apply in future to any aspect of education. It is also possible to reconstruct Canada's policy in other trade negotiations, such as those on the proposed Free Trade Area of the Americas (FTAA) agreement, which is proceeding simultaneously, so that these negotiations also begin to accord with citizens' priorities for education.

None of these things will occur by themselves. Canadians—whether parents, teachers, board members, administrators, students, researchers, or others involved in education; or ordinary citizens—must therefore become actively involved in the GATS debate to ensure that these things **do** occur. They must send the federal government a strong message that our children's education takes precedence over commercial trade interests. In particular, as a first step, citizens must begin by obtaining unequivocal assurances from the federal government that it will fully safeguard our public education system from all GATS rules.

Despite its remoteness from our public education systems, the federal government cannot safely ignore local action. Canada's public schools are rooted in local communities and rely upon the active involvement of citizens—in the classroom, in administrative offices, at school councils, and as elected representatives in local education authorities and provincial governments.

This involvement gives these individuals an intimate knowledge of how our schools work and direct accountability, both of which bring them unique authority when they challenge federal government reassurances about, and approaches to, the GATS. Indeed, federal representatives and officials are plunged into new and uncertain territory, and their current disregard for skeptical views could quickly backfire. They are largely unfamiliar with vast areas of domestic policy that are affected by their negotiating positions, much of which, including public education, falls under provincial and territorial jurisdiction. Their confidence in the presumed adequacy of their cursory consultation exercises belies, at best, an apparent innocence of the political landscape and the dynamics of education.

A brushfire of resistance that starts in school councils and local boards of education could quickly sweep across the country. Not only could this force a shift in the most extreme proposals for GATS expansion, but it could also result in essential changes in federal trade policy and spark further challenges, including to the basis of the GATS itself.

Public education advocates should demand that the federal government back up its oft-stated commitment to safeguarding public education with specific actions; they should also demand clear evidence, including formal positions tabled at the WTO, of the government's actions. Some of these actions Canada can take unilaterally; others require negotiation at the WTO and in other international fora.

6.3.1 Specific changes Canada can make unilaterally

As a primary principle of its trade policy, Canada should seek to "do no harm" to its public education system. Such a precautionary approach, if adopted in the current and future rounds of GATS negotiations, would help protect public education from further GATS pressure and potential challenges in the future.

Canada should make no GATS commitments in any education-related sectors. The federal government should halt plans to negotiate commercial education and training. Whatever commercial benefits could be secured, the risks to public education are too great for Canada to contemplate further subjecting any aspect of the sector to the GATS rules. Therefore, our government should unequivocally inform its WTO negotiating partners, well in advance of the March 31, 2003 deadline for initial offers, that Canada will make no education-related commitments.

Canada should not seek any education-related commitments from other countries. Although technically feasible, seeking GATS commitments in a sector that Canada is determined to safeguard is neither ethically defensible nor practically sustainable as a negotiating position. Canada should clarify its position by indicating, in advance of the June 30, 2002 deadline, that it will make no education-related requests of other WTO member countries.

Federal, provincial and territorial governments should conduct a thorough assessment of the implications of Canada's existing commitments for education, health and social services before Canada makes any further GATS proposals in any sector. This is necessary to address the numerous concerns raised in this report, and elsewhere by concerned citizens.

In each of these areas, action at the community level, in concert with local initiatives elsewhere, could prove especially effective as a critical catalyst for federal action.

6.3.2 Changes in the GATS that Canada must negotiate with other WTO members

Canada should support a thorough assessment of trade in services at the GATS, and support Southern country demands that an initial assessment be concluded before further negotiations proceed. The GATS requires further negotiations to take into account an assessment of trade in services "in overall terms and on a sectoral basis."[1] To date, Canada and other wealthy countries have largely ignored this requirement. A number of Southern countries, both before and following the Doha ministerial conference, have pressed the need for a thorough assessment before further negotiations begin.[2] Canada should work with these nations to ensure that this commitment is fulfilled.

Canada should propose a general, "horizontal" exception for all measures affecting education, health and

other social services. As noted in this report, country-specific reservations, or limitations to GATS commitments, have serious shortcomings. Most importantly, they can be removed unilaterally by any future government and, once removed, in practical terms are almost certain to never be reinstated. By contrast, general, or horizontal, safeguards are far more permanent fixtures of treaties, since they can be changed only with the unanimous consent of treaty members. Canada should make a strong case that public education systems, and public health and other social service systems, deserve protection that can be expected to survive short-term shifts in ideology and domestic politics.

The current melange of country specific exemptions can only be considered a Band-Aid solution until the more permanent protection of a general exemption is secured. Adding a general exception to the GATS text would thus reinforce the country-specific protections Canada and other countries may enter into their schedules of commitments and would ensure that education services are far less likely to be targeted in future rounds of negotiations. A self-defining exception, written in clear language—modelled on the existing general exception for national security measures—would help prevent commercial interests from using the GATS to restrict public education policy.

Canada should mount a serious negotiating effort to ensure that no so-called "disciplines" are developed in the GATS negotiations on domestic regulation (Article VI.4). As discussed in Chapter 4, non-discriminatory regulations, which are complex and constantly being adapted to rapidly changing circumstances, are an essential aspect of democratic governance in public education and other critical areas, and should not be constrained by

GATS rules. In the event other countries ultimately agree to such restrictions, Canada should shield this country's public education system from their application.

Canada should also insist on changes to the "governmental authority" exclusion so that its meaning is clarified, and, critically, that it is made fully effective. Our report has documented the extent of confusion and misinformation within our government regarding this crucial provision. Real changes are needed to ensure that it fully excludes education, health care, and other mixed public-commercial services from the GATS. Canada must not participate in, and must use its considerable influence to prevent, a regrettable alternative: making cosmetic changes designed to mislead the public while cynically and deliberately leaving the narrow scope of the exclusion unaltered.

6.3.3 Beyond the GATS

Concurrently, Canada should work to ensure that its international commitments to the right to education take precedence over trade obligations. As discussed in Chapter 1 of this report, Canada has been a leading proponent of international human rights law, which includes the right to education. The Universal Declaration of Human Rights and the International Covenant on Economic, Social and Cultural Rights oblige signatory governments to ensure equitable access to primary and secondary education. The GATS and other WTO treaties should be amended to stipulate that the right to education, and other international human rights, take precedence in the event of a conflict between trade and human rights obligations. Such an amendment would help to reconcile international trade law with other bodies of international law, in accordance with the Vienna Convention on the Law of Treaties.

Canada should support other international initiatives to remove education from the commercial market and establish a more equitable basis for international exchange of knowledge and learning. Knowledge is a truly social creation that can rarely be attributed to a single individual. The Internet and other technologies offer enormous potential for expanding access globally. Access to knowledge and its benefits should be as free as possible, unfettered by expansive commercial trade rules. Just as Canada is doing in the cultural sphere, it should advocate for an international legal framework for promoting the exchange of knowledge and education outside of trade rules.

Canada should also embark on a reform of its trade policy- making by opening up the negotiating process to full participation and public scrutiny. The country's trade negotiators generally consider their primary mandate to be expanding export markets. They often do not appreciate, and cannot be expected to understand, the intricacies of the public education system without more direct involvement by education professionals, advocates, and the general public. These individuals must not be involved in mere ritualistic, *pro forma* consultations, but in providing serious and valued input towards the formulation of Canada's negotiating position.

Like other international treaties, the GATS is negotiated by the federal government, though it covers many matters that are the jurisdiction of the provinces. The more active participation of provincial education officials in the negotiation process would also help prevent many potential problems for the domestic education sector. Finally, any genuine public consultation process must lead to genuine trade policy reform. If public debate exposes the GATS as an unbalanced or fundamentally undemocratic legal instrument, then it must be either be fundamentally changed or discarded.

6.3.4 Getting started

As a practical matter, there exists a crucial prerequisite to achieving progress in countering the myriad GATS threats to education. Right at the start, it is necessary for public education advocates to overcome a quite understandable sense of disbelief. It is difficult to grasp—both intellectually and emotionally—the full scope of the GATS and its impacts, and the significance of what is being proposed in Geneva. But citizens are almost certain, ultimately, to grasp this. Many already understand that, far from being immune, aspects of the country's public education system are already subject to certain GATS rules. Many more will come to realize that the sector—like all other sectors—is subject to ongoing, repeated negotiations with a view to facilitating corporate, for-profit international business in education by constraining government regulation. At that juncture, public education advocates—working together, and with colleagues in other sectors and other countries—will be in a position to begin to engage on the threats posed by the treaty.

Fortunately, knowledge about that the GATS is no longer restricted to treaty proponents or trade specialists, but is growing among divergent types of individuals, in many countries, and in a variety of sectors. There are many organizations, including those involved in the publication of this report, that are now actively involved in the GATS debate. The threats the treaty poses to public services—including but not limited to education—are beginning to attract increasing amounts of public attention world-wide. It seems only a matter of time before the general haze of debilitating disinformation and disbelief surrounding the GATS is blown away by the stark realization of citizens throughout the world of just how far, and in what direction, GATS negotiators have been allowed to proceed.

One of the first priorities for citizens concerned about the GATS is to demand accountability from responsible elected representatives. This can take many forms, ranging from questions from parents at local school boards, motions passed by union locals or local parent organizations, to representations made to provincial and national organizations, and to oral and written public inquiries of provincial education ministers, trade ministers, premiers, and prime ministers.

Without overlooking the obvious and important role of trade negotiators, trade bureaucrats and other officials, it is important to avoid focusing exclusively on their role. Their political masters, our elected representatives, must be brought to account for the responsibility they have in relation to the GATS.

It is equally important not to treat trade ministers, or trade ministries, as unaccountable. Rather, they should be treated as any other minister or department that needs to be called to account for transgressions into areas outside their legitimate authority.

There are significant grounds for optimism that efforts to counter the GATS will ultimately prove effective. One of the most potent tools public education advocates have at their disposal is the growing recognition among trade activists that well-organized groups of concerned citizens can have real influence in international negotiations. Indeed, recent evidence indicates that such influence can have salutary, even dramatic effects, not merely on the details of a particular treaty, but on the fate of the treaty itself. As Sinclair[3] notes:

"In late 1998 the proposed Multilateral Agreement on Investment (MAI), an agreement that shared the GATS excessive reach and whose proponents exhibited a similar overweening ambition, suffered a stunningly unexpected defeat largely at the hands of a well-informed, sophisticated and organized international citizenry. In Seattle in late 1999, deep-seated public opposition was a critical factor in turning back plans by the WTO to launch a new 'millenium round' of comprehensive negotiations."

While it is true that the subsequent attempt to launch a new round of WTO negotiations was successful, this was achieved only through coercion and arm-twisting, was more limited than many proponents desired, and remains controversial. Similarly, some major media outlets have contended that the tragic events at New York's World Trade Center altered the nature of the trade debate and placed the WTO critics on the defensive. What is seldom noted, however, is that recent revelations about the Enron collapse have shaken many citizens' faith in large-scale deregulation and may have reinforced long-standing concerns about close ties between politicians and those in the business world.

Moreover, as discussed in Chapter 3 of this report, the reputation of Edison Schools—the United States' preeminent for-profit education management organization—has been severely tarnished. It stands accused of knowingly misleading investors by exaggerating its revenue stream. The company has seen its stock price collapse and a raft of class action suits commenced against its senior executives. Coming hard on the heels of the Enron debacle, the example of the for-profit Edison Schools, Inc.

serves to clarify the distinction between private, corporate insider interests on the one hand, and, on the other, the interests of all of our children, and the future of our public education system.

This distinction between private corporate interests and the public interests that are reflected in Canada's public education system is, as we have seen in this report, made even more starkly by the GATS. We are rapidly approaching:
- the June 30, 2002 deadline for Canada to make requests of other countries, and for Canada to receive *other* countries' requests for market openings in *our* education services sector, and
- the March 31, 2003 deadline for Canada, and other countries, to expand the reach of the GATS by making additional specific commitments under the treaty.

The active involvement in the GATS debate by public education advocates throughout Canada—in every community and school district, and in every province and territory—is as urgent as it is critical.

Endnotes

Introduction

[1] This section title is drawn from a recent paper, published by the OECD, that is designed to reassure the public about the GATS and education. In fact, the paper is far from reassuring. While denigrating critics and their concerns, it reiterates many of the misleading claims that have appeared elsewhere, which are considered in this report.
Sauvé, Pierre, *Trade, Education and the GATS: What's in, what's out, what's all the fuss about*, Organization for Economic Co-operation and Development, Paper prepared for the OECD/US Forum on Trade in Educational Services, 23-24 May 2002, Washington, D.C., USA.

Chapter 1

[1] WTO Secretariat, Trade in Services Division, *An Introduction to the GATS*, Geneva, October, 1999, p. 1.
[2] Global Services Network (1999) Recommendations of the Global Services Network and Business Policy Forums for Services 2000 Trade Negotiations, World Services Congress, Atlanta, November 1-3, 1999; in Stern, Robert, ed. (2001) *Services in the International Economy*, Ann Arbor, University of Michigan Press, pp. 461-482.
[3] Sinclair, Scott and Grieshaber-Otto, Jim (2002) *Facing the Facts: A guide to the GATS debate*, Ottawa, Canadian Centre for Policy Alternatives, available online at http://www.policyalternatives.ca .
[4] The following documents provide valuable introductions to the GATS:
- World Trade Organization Training Package, *Services: GATS*, 15 December 1998, available at http://www.wto.org/wto/services/services.htm .
- Sinclair, Scott (2000) *How the World Trade Organization's new 'services' negotiations threaten democracy*, Ottawa: Canadian Centre for Policy Alternatives.

5   Howse, Robert and Mutua, Makau (2000) *Protecting Human Rights in a Global Economy: Challenges for the World Trade Organization*, available at http://www.ichrdd.ca/english/commdoc/publications/globalization/wtoRightsGlob.html. In elaborating on their assertions, these authors state: "Unlike treaty law, which is based on the consent of states, customary international law binds all states. Customary international law 'results from a general and consistent practice of states followed by them out of a sense of legal obligation.' Thus customary international law binds all states without exception and irrespective of their consent. In contrast, international treaty law only binds those states that have given their express consent to the treaty or agreement in question. For human rights, this distinction is critical because the location of a human rights norm in either source changes its status in international law and could constitute the difference between an automatically binding obligation and a voluntary commitment. Customary international law, unlike treaty law, must be obeyed by states, their wishes notwithstanding."
They note also that "the UN Committee on Economic, Social and Cultural Rights has written that trade liberalization, 'must be understood as a means, not an end. The end which trade liberalization should serve is the objective of human well-being to which the international human rights instruments give legal expression.'"

6   Article 31. This treaty may be accessed at http://www.un.org/law/ilc/texts/treaties.htm.

7   It is noteworthy, therefore, that the 1994 Marrakesh Agreement Establishing the World Trade Organization, which is the supreme legislation governing the interpretation of all WTO trade agreements, makes no reference to the UDHR, nor to the Charter of the United Nations, nor to the Vienna Convention on the Law of Treaties. The legal regime established by the Marrakesh Agreement, which includes the powerful WTO Dispute Settlement Mechanism, nowhere explicitly recognizes that trade rules are subordinate to, or at very least must take into account, fundamental human rights and the obligations they confer on national governments.

8   Howse and Mutua, op. cit..

9   Updates on this case (case #27418) — together with transcripts of interventions made by such groups as the Canadian Asssociation of Statutory Human Rights Agencies (Cashra), the Charter Committee on Poverty Issues (CCPI), the National Association of Women and the Law (NAWL), and Rights and Democracy — are available on the website of the Supreme Court of Canada at http://www.scc-csc.gc.ca or, more specifically, at http://209.47.227.134/scripts/hsrun.hse/haht51/SCC CASE/SCC CASE.htx; start=HS_scc_case?lang=0.
10 The commercial bias inherent in applying trade rules to education services does not in itself conflict with the right to education. Under international human rights law, however, national governments have the obligation to ensure that elementary education is freely available to all, and that education at all levels is directed to the objectives set out in article 26 of the Universal Declaration. Commercialization or privatization appear to conflict with the right to education, therefore, when they impede or derogate from the ability of Canadian governments to fulfill these fundamental obligations.
11 United Nations Committee on Economic, Social and Cultural Rights, Implementation of the International Covenant on Economic, Social and Cultural Rights: General Comment no.13, the right to education, 8 December 1999, E/C.12/1999/10, CESCR, paragraph 13.
12 Ibid., paragraph 6.
13 Ibid., paragraph 45.
14 Ibid., paragraph 47.
15 Ibid., paragraph 54.
16 See: Dommen, Caroline, (2002) "Raising Human Rights Concerns in the World Trade Organisation: Actors, Processes and Possible Strategies", *Human Rights Quarterly*, Vol. 24, No. 1 available online, by subscription, at http://muse.jhu.edu/journals/human_rights_quarterly/
and
Bronson, Diana and Lamarche, Lucie, (2001) *A Human Rights Framework for Trade in the Americas*, Rights and Democracy, Montreal, March, available online at http://serveur.ichrdd.ca/english/commdoc/publications/globalization/FTAA/frameworkFinal.html.

17 The text of the bill —Bill 45 – Responsible Choice for Growth and Accountability Act (Budget 2001) – can be found at http://www.ontla.on.ca/documents/Bills/37_Parliament/Session2/index-01.htm#P403_30099. The government's news release, containing its description its so-called Equity in Education Tax Credit, passed on December 17, 2001, is found at http://www.newswire.ca/government/ontario/english/releases/December2001/17/c7595.html.
18 Article 26(3).
19 Article 13(3-4).
20 ICESCR, General Comment no.13, op.cit., paragraph 54.

Chapter 2

1 GATS Article XXVIII(a)
2 cf. Article I:3(a)
3 These all-inclusive modes of delivery are referred to, in the order of the examples cited, as (mode 1) cross-border supply, (mode 2) consumption abroad, (mode 3) commercial presence and (mode 4) presence of natural persons. They are set out in Article I:2(a)-(d).
4 This principle has been described in the following terms: "[t]he object of the GATS it to prevent governments from distinguishing between *like* services and service providers based on the particular mode through which the services are supplied. A service consumed by a citizen abroad is the same, for regulatory purposes, as one consumed locally.... And a service provided over the phone or the internet is the same, for regulatory purposes, as one provided through a locally established subsidiary." (Sinclair, Scott, *GATS: How the World Trade Organization's new 'services' negotiations threaten democracy*, Ottawa: Canadian Centre for Policy Alternatives, 2001, pp. 44-5).
5 The WTO Secretariat's GATS Training Package, released in 1998, notes (p. 10) that "[t]his wide definition of trade in services makes the GATS directly relevant to many areas of regulation which traditionally have not been touched upon by multilateral trade rules."
6 WTO GATS Training Package, op. cit., p. 9.

[7] Article I:1 states: "This Agreement applies to measures by Members affecting trade in services."
[8] EC: Bananas, Panel Report, para. 7.280; cited in Sinclair (2000), p. 41.
[9] Sinclair (2001), op. cit., p. 41.
[10] *GATS and Public Service Systems: The GATS 'governmental authority' exclusion is narrower than it first appears, may undergo urgent review*, discussion paper, Ministry of Employment and Investment, Government of British Columbia, Canada, April 2, 2001. This paper originally appeared at http://www.ei.gov.bc.ca/Trade&Export/FTAA-WTO/WTO/governmentalauth.htm and is now available at http://members.iinet.net.au/~jenks/GATS_BC2001.html Krajewski, Markus, Public Services and the Scope of the General Agreement on Trade in Services, research paper, Center for International Environmental Law (CIEL), May 2001. (available at http://www.xs4all.nl/~ceo/gatswatch/markus.html).
[11] For example, as considered further in Chapter 5, the Canadian government asserts in its website that "Basic education … services … are … not covered by the GATS." The UK Minister for Trade stated in a letter to a fellow MP in November 2000 that "[w]e are clear that GATS does not apply to services provided by central and local governments". And the Saskatchewan minister of Post-Secondary Education and Skills Training recently wrote "I am advised that the current GATS excludes public services from its scope". (The latter two examples are cited in *GATS and Public Service Systems*, op. cit., footnote 20.)
[12] As the British Columbia Government's discussion paper points out (pp. 5-6), the GATS exemption to protect "essential security interests" (Article XIVbis) is unique in that it is self-defined and very broad. Other exceptions including, for example, the exemption to "protect human, animal or plant life or health" (Article XIV) are subject to strict limitations.
[13] Section 1, p.5.
[14] The GATS preamble states: "*Recognizing* the right of Members to regulate, and to introduce new regulations, on the supply of services within their territories in order to meet national policy objectives…" Counterbalancing this reference, in the preamble itself, are the references in support of "pro-

gressive liberalization" and, subsequently, "progressively higher levels of liberalization ... through successive rounds of ... negotiations."

15 This point is considered in greater detail in Sinclair and Grieshaber-Otto, *Facing the Facts*, 2002, op. cit..

16 *GATS and Public Service Systems*, British Columbia Government discussion paper, op. cit., pp. 11-12.

17 Working Party on GATS Rules, Report of the Meeting of 6 October 1998, Note by the Secretariat, S/WPGR/M/18, 13 November 1998, p. 4. Cited in *GATS and Public Service Systems*, op. cit., p. 11.

18 Working Party on GATS Rules, Report of the Meeting of 19 February 1999, Note by the Secretariat, S/WPGR/M/20, 17 March 1999, p. 7. Cited in *GATS and Public Service Systems*, op. cit., p. 11.

19 The then-director of the WTO Services Division told the European Services Forum in November 2000 that "we in the [WTO] Secretariat often have to explain the exclusion of governmental services and we have come up against the difficulty that these terms are not further defined. We need to be clear on what is meant by 'not on a commercial basis'." Hartridge, David, Conference on GATS 2000 Negotiations, European Services Forum, Brussels, 27 November, 2000. Cited in *GATS and Public Service Systems*, op. cit., p. 11.

20 Education Services, Background Note by the Secretariat, Council for Trade in Services, 29 September 1998, S/C/W/49, p. 4. Cited in *GATS and Public Service Systems*, op. cit., p. 14.

21 *GATS and Public Service Systems*, op. cit., pp. 6-7.

22 Health and Social Services, Background Note by the Secretariat, Council for Trade in Services, 18 September 1998, S/C.W/50, pp. 10-11. Cited in *GATS and Public Service Systems*, op. cit., p. 13.

23 Council for Trade in Services, Report of the Meeting Held on 14 October 1998, Note by the Secretariat, S/C/M/30, 12 November 1998, p. 4. Cited in *GATS and Public Service Systems*, op. cit., pp. 12-13.

24 According to the then-director of the WTO Services Division, "The original proposal to make it clear that governmental services were not covered [in the Uruguay Round GATS] came from the EU and it was not controversial." Hartridge,

Perilous Lessons 161

David, Conference on GATS 2000 Negotiations, European Services Forum, Brussels, 27 November 2000, p. 2. The proposal by the European Community, made in a 1990 communication to the WTO, states: "ARTICLE I:3. The provisions of this Agreement shall not apply to an activity whenever it consists of the exercise of official authority." (Proposal by the European Community, Draft General Agreement on Trade in Services, Communication from the European Communities, 18 June 1990, MTN.GNS/W/105.)

[25] European Communities, Joint Communication from the Parties, Committee on Regional Trade Agreements, WT/REG50/2/Add.3; WT/REG51/2/Add.3; WT/REG52/2/Add.3 19 May 1999, Item 3, para. 3. Cited in *GATS and Public Service Systems*, op. cit., p. 8.

[26] Ibid., para. 6

[27] Some WTO officials have recently commented on the significance of the GATS governmental authority exclusion. (See for example, World Trade Organization, Trade in Services Secretariat, *GATS: Fact and Fiction*, Geneva, March 2001, available on the WTO website at http://www.wto.org).

However, the primary aim of these remarks has apparently not been to eliminate the threats that the current narrow exclusion now poses to education and other public service systems. Instead, the main goals appear to have been to belittle GATS critics, deny the existence of a problem, and solicit the support of GATS proponents. The ultimate aim of these interventions is apparently to ensure that the existing GATS exclusion remains very narrow and, to that end, to prevent controversy surrounding the treaty's coverage of public service systems from undermining ongoing negotiations to broaden and deepen the treaty.

A critique of recent WTO and OECD rejoinders against GATS critics is contained in Sinclair and Grieshaber-Otto, *Facing the Facts*, 2002, op. cit..

[28] Gould, Ellen & Joy, Clare, *In whose service? The threat posed by the General Agreement on Trade in Services to economic development in the South*, World Development Movement Report, December, 2000, Part II, para. 1. (available at http://www.wdm.org.uk/cambriefs/WTO/Inwhoseservice.htm).

[29] Sinclair, 2000, op. cit., p. 2.

30 Provisional Central Product Classification, 1991, New York, United Nations, p. vi. (ST/ESA/STAT/SER.M/77) (available online at http://esa.un.org/unsd/cr/registry/regrt.asp)
31 United Nations Statistics Division website, May, 2001. (From http://esa.un.org/unsd/cr/registry/regrt.asp, select CPCprov, then Profile, then Remarks.)
32 The United Nations Statistic Division refers to this document on its website as the "GNS/120", but it appears to be more commonly referred to as the "W/120". It is dated 10 July 1991and appears under the WTO code MTN.GNS/W/120.
33 The subcategories and descriptions noted below are found in the CPC and not in the less detailed W/120.
34 The vast majority of the following CPC categories are substantially similar to those contained in the revised CPC, known as the CPC V1.0, which supersedes it for UN classification purposes and which could eventually form the basis for the classification of services in future GATS negotiations.
35 New Zealand proposes a change to specify that the 'academic study and teaching of sport and recreational activities' is classified as education rather than sporting services. *Communication from New Zealand*, op.cit., paragraph 10.
36 It is not always obvious into which category a particular service will be classified for the purposes of the GATS. In the event of a GATS dispute relating to classification, the matter will be resolved by a dispute settlement panel.
37 Sinclair, S. (2001) *The GATS and Canadian Postal Services* (Ottawa, Canadian Centre for Policy Alternatives; available at http://www.policyalternatives.ca).
38 See, for example, Warren, T. & Findlay, C (1999) How significant are the barriers? Measuring impediments to trade in services, paper presented at the 'Services 2000: New Directions in Services Trade Liberalization' conference at the University Club in Washington, D.C., 1-2 June 1999.
39 World Trade Organization (1997) *EC - Regime for The Importation, Sale and Distribution of Bananas*, Report of the Appellate Body, 09.09.97, WT/DS27/AB/R, para. 234.
40 Sinclair, S. (2000) op. cit., p. 44.
41 Canada, Schedule of Specific Commitments, General Agreement on Trade in Services, 15 April 1994, GATS/SC/16. Note that specific commitments may not apply to all services in the listed categories.

42 Grieshaber-Otto, J., Sinclair, S. & Schacter, N. (2000) Impacts of international trade, services and investment treaties on alcohol regulation, *Addiction*, Supplement 4, p. S501.
43 Sinclair, S. (2000) op. cit., p. 76.
44 Swenarchuk, M (2000) *General Agreement on Trade in Services: negotiations concerning Domestic Regulations under GATS Article VI(4); Submitted to the Department of Foreign Affairs and International Trade and to Industry Canada*, (Canadian Environmental Law Association).

Chapter 3

1 Authors' calculation from data reported in source: Council of Ministers of Education, Canada, *Education Indicators in Canada: report of the pan-Canadian education indicators project 1999*, tables 3.22, 3.23 and 3.26.
2 People for Education, *The 2001 Tracking Study*, June 2001, pp. 12, 48-49. (Available from People for Education, P.O. Box 64, Station P, Toronto, M5S 2S6 or online at http://ww.peopleforeducation.com).
3 Ibid
4 Ibid, p.12.
5 Examples in this section are from Andrew Stark, What's Wrong with Private Funding for Public Schools? in *Dissent*, 19 January 2001.
6 Stark, op.cit.
7 Peter McLaughlin, Wal-Mart school adoptees profiting, *The Halifax Daily News*, Monday, January 8, 2001.
8 Janet Steffenhagen, Delta board to allow more advertising in schools, *The Vancouver Sun* Friday, 19 Jan 2001, p. B3.
9 Robert Barron, Schools seek Germans, Russians; District sends representative on Team Canada trip to Europe, hoping to recruit students to Nanaimo, *Daily News*, February 20, 2002, p. A3.
10 Information taken from the "Study in Canada!" web site: http://www.studyincanada.com .
11 Ibid
12 CEC Network 1998/1999 Annual Report http://ww.cecnetwork.org). CEC staff estimate that actual numbers of foreign students entering Canada may be as high as dou-

ble these figures, because students taking short-term language courses are not required to obtain immigration authorization.

[13] Gardner Wilson (Director of Public Policy and Research, CEC Networks), personal communication with Matthew Sanger, 25 June 2001.

[14] WTO Council for Trade in Services, Communication from New Zealand (S/CSS/W/93) p.3.

[15] Canadian Union of Public Employees, "Public Risk, Private Profit: why lease-back schools are bad for K-12 education" (undated, available on www.cupe.ca).

[16] See: Jeff Holubitsky, "IGA school a go, like it or not, province says: Alberta would back plan over objections from city council", Edmonton Journal, June 23, 2001, p. B3.
Sheila Pratt, Shopping-cart school idea gets failing grade: Edmonton's newly elected Tories should fight for what's best for city, not government, *Edmonton Journal*, July 14, 2001, p. H3.
Bill Mah, School-store scheme runs into land-use dispute: Catholic board caught between city and provincial rules, *Edmonton Journal*, February 12, 2002, Final Edition, p. B1.

[17] In June, 2001, reportedly due largely to concerns about the application of NAFTA and GATS rules, the Greater Vancouver Regional District water district board backed out of a plan to privatize the operation of a multi-million dollar water filtration plant for the city's Seymour and Capilano reservoirs.

[18] A recent legal opinion considers these issues:
Shrybman, Steven, *A Legal Opinion Concerning the Potential Impact of International Trade Disciplines on Proposals to Establish A Public-Private Partnership to Design Build and Operate a Water Filtration Plant in the Seymour Reservoir*, Prepared for the Canadian Union of Public Employees, Sack Goldblatt Mitchell, Toronto, May 31, 2001. (summary available at http://www.cupe.ca/issues/privatization/showitem.asp?ID=3699; full text from the authors).

[19] Lawrence Hardy, "Mental Help", in *American School Board Journal* (January 2001), pp.33-35.

[20] Pat Macadie and Erika Shaker, "Putting ETS to the Test", CCPA Education Project, Corporate Profiles, v.1,n.1, June 20, 2001. Available at http://www.policyalternatives.ca.

[21] NCITE website, http://www.tradeineducation.org/general_iinfo/intro.html. Sylvan Learning Systems is also an NCITE member; see http://www.tradeineducation.org/general_info/founding_members.html.
[22] Communication from the United States, W/CSS/W/23, op. cit., paras 2, 4 and 6.
[23] Andrew Nikiforuk, Zapped!, *National Post Business Magazine*, May 2001, pp. 89-95.
[24] Steven Downes, News Trolls, Inc., quoted in Polaris Institute corporate profile, November 28, 2000. (http://www.polarisinstitute.org).
[25] Other communications companies are also involved in the education sector. For example, Shaw Cable is reportedly giving about $500,000 toward a new "telelearning centre" at Edmonton's Percy Page high school. The company has been providing the school fast communications connection, worth an estimated $5,000 per month, for the last two years.
Holubitsky, Jeff, Opening school doors to sponsors: Approval of school, grocery store raises many possibilities: THIS SCHOOL IS BROUGHT TO YOU BY ..., *Edmonton Journal*, July 3, 2001, Final Edition, p. B1.
[26] Le triomphe du privé, *L'actualité*, 15 November 2000, pp 42-46.
[27] Ontario Ministry of Finance, Budget supports equity in education, press release, 9 May 2001. http://www.gov.on.ca/fin).
[28] In the interest of clarity, this report consistently uses the latter phrase.
[29] Molnar, A.; Morales, J. & Vander Wyst, A. (2000) Profiles of For-Profit Education Management Companies 1999-2000, Center for the Analysis of Commercialism in Education (CACE), School of Education, University of Wisconsin-Milwaukee, pp. 1-2. http://www.asu.edu/educ/epsl/CERU/CERU_2000_Research_Writing.htm).
[30] See, for example: *Politics, Markets and America's Schools* (1990) by [Edison Chief Education Officer] John E. Chubb with Terry M. Moe; *The Market Approach to Education* (1999) by John F. Witte, Jr.; *School Choice and Social Controversy: Politics, Policy, and Law* by Stephen D. Sugarman and Frank R. Kemerer, eds. (2000); and *The Great School Debate: Choice, Vouchers, and Charters* (2000) by Thomas L. Good and Jennifer S. Braden. A use-

ful profile of conservative education economist Caroline Hoxby recently appeared in the New Yorker magazine. Cassidy, John, Schools are Her Business, *The New Yorker*, October 18 & 25, 1999, pp. 144-160.

31 Actual voucher schemes often diverge from the model. For instance Florida's voucher system, initiated in 1999, is targeted at students in 'chronically failing' schools. See: Fact Sheet on Education Vouchers, Elementary Teachers Federation of Ontario, May 2001. (available at http://www.etfo.on.ca).

32 Molnar et al., op. cit., p. 1.

33 Ibid.

34 Ibid., pp. 3-4.

35 Bracey, Gerald, "The Market in Theory Meets the Market in Practice: The Case of Edison Schools", Education Policy Research Unit (EPRU), Education Policy Studies Laboratory, College of Education, Arizona State University, February, 2002. This 11-page report provides a valuable critique of the Edison School project and its recent history in the United States. It is available online at http://www.asu.edu/educ/epsl/Reports/epru/EPRU%202002-107/EPSL-0202-107-EPRU.htm.

36 Coalition for Public Education, pamphlet OSDOO-0067, February, 2000.

37 Thompson, Rachel, "Formula approaches to improving GATS commitments: Some options for negotiators", paper prepared for the *Services 2000: New Directions in Services Trade Liberalization* conference, sponsored by the American Enterprise Institute, the Brookings Institution, the Center for Business and Government, Harvard University, and the CSI Research and Education Foundation, Washington, D.C., 1-2 June 1999.

38 Measures affecting trade and investment in education services in the Asia-Pacific region, Report to the APEC Group on Services 2000, APEC Secretariat, December, 2000 (available at http://www.apecsec.org.sg/)

39 S/CSS/W/93; op. cit.

40 Negotiating Proposal for Education Services, Communication from Australia, Council for Trade in Services, Special Session, 1 October 2001, S/CSS/W/110.

41 Ibid., para. 7.

42 Ibid., para. 8(a).

[43] Ibid., para. 8(c).
[44] Council for Trade in Services, Education Services: Background note by the Secretariat, S/C/W/49, 23 September 1998, p. 4.
[45] In the short-term, the impact of GATS on higher education is likely to attract greater attention, presumably due largely to the perception of a greater potential for commercial gain. As one example of this greater interest, the OECD and the United States Government have organized a forum on "Trade in Educational Services" for May 23-24, 2002 in Washington, D.C..
[46] Global Services Network, Statement on WTO Negotiations on Services, November 1999, p. 1. Cited in Sinclair, 2000, p. 9.
[47] ETS has recently been contracted by the Ontario government to develop the entrance to the profession test for prospective teachers. Patricia McAdie, Putting ETS to the Test, CCPA Education Project, Corporate Profile vol.1.no.1, June 20, 2001.
[48] It must be acknowledged here that this analysis is based on the generous assumption, perhaps unwarranted, that the government authority exclusion is, at least to some degree, effective.
[49] GATS Impact on Education in Canada, Legal Opinion, Gottlieb & Pearson, October 2001, p. 12.
[50] It is of interest to note that Canadian finance department officials have, in a different context, decried the lack of clarity of a related concept, that of "directly competitive services". They note in a 1999 paper that
"The ... problem we would have to sort out is what constitutes 'like or directly competitive services'. The very nature of services trade makes this determination somewhat more tenuous since so much of what is delivered as a service is custom-tailored to meet the needs of the consumer of the service. In addition, the intangible nature of service provision creates difficulties in trying to compare a foreign service to a domestic service. Moreover, the concept of 'like or directly competitive' would be made considerably more complicated if we were to have to determine whether a service supplied cross boarder was similar to one supplied through one of the other modes of supply."
(Safeguards and Subsidy Disciplines in Services Trade: Déjà Vu or New Beginning, Gilles Gauthier, in collaboration with Erin O'Brien and Susan Spencer. Draft paper presented at the *Services 2000: New Directions in Services Trade Liberaliza-*

tion Conference at the University Club in Washington, D.C., 1-2 June 1999, p. 8.) The notion of "like" services, particularly in the context of services delivered via the internet, remains controversial and is considered briefly in a subsequent section.

More generally, Gould and Schacter have described how a WTO panel ruling involving alcohol regulation gave a broad interpretation of what constitute "like" or "directly competitive or substitutable" products for purposes of applying WTO national treatment provisions. (Ellen Gould and Noel Schacter, "Trade liberalization and its impacts on alcohol policy", *SAIS Review 22.1*, Winter-Spring 2002, Johns Hopkins University Press, available, by subscription, at http://muse.jhu.edu/journals/sais_review/toc/sais22.1.html). Determining what constitutes a service that is "in competition with" another thus appears to be fraught with difficulty. In the event of a GATS dispute, this determination will be made by a WTO dispute settlement panel on a case by case basis, and it seems likely that panels will interpret the concept at least as broadly as its ordinary definition, especially as the services or providers in question do not need to be "like" to be competing.

[51] Once again, it is important to recognize that this analysis may give too much credence to the view that the governmental authority exclusion is fairly broad. But even if one takes what to public services advocates would be an optimistic view, this analysis suggests that it is almost certainly not possible to "ring fence", or completely protect, public services from GATS provisions. Even a modest degree of commercialization or privatization in the sector would likely make the exclusion apply in a very narrow range of services.

[52] Article XXVIII, setting out GATS definitions, specifies that the establishment of 'commercial presence' (one of the four modes of service supply), includes establishment through a 'juridical person'. It defined 'juridical person' as *"any legal entity* duly constituted or otherwise organized under applicable law, *whether for profit or otherwise,* and *whether privately-owned or governmentally-owned…"* (Article XXVIII (d) and (l); emphasis added).

In addition, the market access provisions, which apply where Members undertake specific commitments, prohibit "measures which restrict or require specific types of legal entity ... through which a service supplier may supply a service..." (Article XVI:2(e)

53 In essence, this requirement amounts to a limited and modified form of 'top-down' application of specific commitments, where such commitments would apply to all services, in all modes of supply, whether for-profit or not for profit, *unless specifically excluded.*

54 For example, Canadian negotiators appear to have "made more than one mistake by failing to properly exclude the Auto Pact provisions from the GATS." (cf. Sinclair, 2000, op. cit., pp. 52-3.)

55 "Frequently asked questions about the GATS," The GATS, public services, health and education, http:// strategis.ic.gc.ca/SSG/sk00100e.html#general , updated May 25, 2001.

56 The DFAIT website indicates that according to the federal government, the so-called "knowledge industry" includes "the delivery of on-line courseware and programs via technology-mediated and distance learning models, procurement of contracts for education and training funded by International Financial Institutions (IFIs) such as the World Bank, exporting of corporate training and educational products, and recruitment of international students to study in Canada." http://www.dfait-maeci.gc.ca/ics-cki/menu-e.asp.

57 Cf. World Education Market website: http://www.wemex.com .

58 Bill 34, *School Amendment Act,* 2002. See, for example, section 27 and part 6.1 "Companies". The bill is available online at http://www.legis.gov.bc.ca/37th3rd/1st_read/gov34-1.htm.

59 Two prominent GATS proponents have also drawn attention to the tendency of GATT negotiators to trade off domestic regulations to obtain concessions for export interests:
"[T]he process of liberalizing trade in goods through reciprocal negotiations under GATT auspices has been successful because the intrinsically mercantilist behavior of trade negotiators (who focus exclusively on obtaining better access to export market for their national industries, using domestic trade barriers as negotiating coin)..."

(Liberalizing Trade in Services: From Reciprocal Negotiation to Domestic Regulatory Reform, Bernard Hoekman and Patrick A. Meserlin, Draft paper presented at the Services 2000: New Directions in Services Trade Liberalization Conference at the University Club in Washington, D.C., 1-2 June 1999, p. 3.)

60 GATS – Fact and Fiction, WTO Secretariat, 2001, p. 7. (available at http://ww.wto.org)
61 Sinclair and Grieshaber-Otto, 2002, op. cit..
62 Only energy services has attracted fewer GATS specific commitments. Education Services, Background Note by the Secretariat, S/C/W/49, op. cit., p. 10.
63 For a detailed analysis of these claims, see Sinclair and Grieshaber-Otto, 2002, op. cit. Among other things, this analysis criticizes GATS proponents' common assurances that the treaty "recognizes the right of Members to regulate" as being "terribly misleading".
64 This section draws on Sinclair and Grieshaber-Otto, 2002, op. cit..
65 These issues also apply to other GATS obligations including, most notably, national treatment.
66 Council for Trade in Services, Work Programme on Electronic Commerce, *Interim Report to the General Council*, 31 March 1999, S/C/8, p. 5.
67 In its March 1999 interim report to the General Council on electronic commerce, the Council for Trade in Services notes that "In no case should any record of this interim report be used to imply that a final view has been reached on any issue; all remain open for further discussion." However, the Council highlighted a number of issues "on which a common understanding appeared to be emerging." The Council's subsequent progress report reiterates these items, identifying them, rather more definitely, as "[p]oints of common understanding". The issues considered here are among those for which general agreement among members appears to have been reached.
Council for Trade in Services, op. cit., S/C/8, pp. 1-2, paras. 3, 4.
Trade in Services, Work Programme on Electronic Commerce, *Progress Report to the General Council*, Adopted by the Coun-

cil for Trade in Services on 19 July 1999, 27 July 1999, S/L/74, p. 1, para. 3.
68 Council for Trade in Services, S/C/8, op. cit., pp. 1-2, para. 4.
69 Council for Trade in Services, *Report of the Meeting Held on 3 December 2001*, Note by the Secretariat, 25 January 2002, S/C/M/56, p. 5, para. 28. Italics added and formatting altered for clarity.
70 Emphasis added; Trade in Services, S/L/74, op. cit., p. 2, para. 8.
71 Emphasis added; Trade in Services, S/L/74, op. cit., p. 3, paras. 15, 17.
72 Electronic delivery of education services is likely to become increasingly common, and some companies naturally anticipate this with enthusiasm. For example, John Chambers, ECO of Cisco Systems has proclaimed that the "next big killer application for the Internet is going to be education. Education over the Internet is going to be so big it is going to make e-mail look like a rounding error." (Canadian Education Industry Summit 2000 Making It Happen: The Bridging of Education and Private Finance, http://www.nationalpost.com/npevents/conferences.html, accessed October 10, 2000.)
73 The concept of modal neutrality with respect to the MFN obligation is apparently at odds with the ability of members to differentiate between modes in making national treatment commitments. In future rounds of treaty negotiations, the trend towards fuller coverage and a more universal adoption of modal neutrality — including for electronically delivered services — could render this conflict moot. And in such a circumstance, members' ability to protect existing public service systems from the GATS would become markedly more precarious.
74 Ironically, the GATS transparency provisions could be used to expose *restrictions* on vending machines. By contrast, the terms of long-term exclusive service contracts designed to ensure the *continued presence* of vending machines would remain secret.
75 Immediately after the conclusion of the WTO Ministerial Meeting in Doha, the European Communities characterized the mandate for negotiating transparency provisions in procurement rules as an essential tool for further liberalization

in that area. "[The] mandate to negotiate ... a multilateral agreement on transparency in government procurement ... [is] a necessary first step that would facilitate further implementation of other international instruments ... such as any development of procurement rules under the GATS or the GPA [Government Procurement Agreement] itself.... [I]t would [also] facilitate bilateral or regional agreements on government procurement or access onto the GPA."
"WTO Ministerial, Doha: Assessment of Results for EU, Memo, Doha, 14 November 2001 (available at http://trade-info.cec.eu.int/europa/2001newround/p14/php)

76 Professor Christopher Findlay, of the Asia Pacific School of Economics and Management at the Australian National University, authored the influential APEC report on trade barriers in education services (see Section 4.3). Measures affecting trade and investment in education services in the Asia-Pacific region, op. cit., p. 7.

77 Warren and Findlay, 1999, How significant are the barriers?, op. cit., p. 1.

78 The GATS Domestic Regulation rules are considered in Chapter 2, section 2.3.3.

79 It is possible, when members understand the full extent of the potential impacts on their regulatory ability, that no such rules will ever be applied. Members could decide that no new GATS regulatory "disciplines" are "necessary" or advisable. However, the current evidence suggests that there have not yet been moves in this direction.

80 Article VIII:5

81 *Services: GATS*, World Trade Organization Training Package, WTO Secretariat, 15 December 1998, p. 23.

82 The issue is considered briefly in Sinclair and Grieshaber-Otto, Facing the Facts, op. cit..

83 We are grateful to Ellen Gould for identifying this important area for future research.

By way of example, Section 36(1) of the Saskatchewan *Trade Union Act* specifies that:

"[u]pon the request of a trade union representing a majority of employees in any appropriate unit, the following clause shall be included in any collective bargaining agreement entered into between that trade union and the employer concerned...:

Every employee who is now or hereafter becomes a member of the union shall maintain his [sic] membership in the union as a condition of his [sic] employment ..."
Under this legislation, failure on the part of any employer to carry out this provision constitutes "an unfair labour practice".
This legislation is available online at http://www.qp.gov.sk.ca/documents/English/Statutes/Statutes/T17.pdf

[84] Canada's specific commitments are found in: *Canada: Schedule of Specific Commitments*, General Agreement on Trade in Services, 15 April 1994, GATS/SC/16, available online at http://www.wto.org.

Chapter 4

[1] Former Trade Commissioner of the European Union, the Right Honourable Lord Brittan of Spennithorne Q.C. is currently Vice-Chairman of the international banking house UBS Warburg Dillon Read. He also chairs the Liberalization of Trade in Services (LOTIS) committee, which recently attracted controversy because it obtained, from UK government officials, confidential GATS negotiating documents and information on the negotiating positions of the European Communities, the US and developing countries. Additional information on these secret meetings, including minutes of their proceedings, is available from CorpWatch (see "The WTO's Hidden Agenda", Greg Palast, November 9, 2001; http://www.corpwatch.org), GATSwatch (http://www.GATSwatch.org) and the Corporate Europe Observatory (http://www.xs4all.nl/~ceo/)

[2] By far the most significant of these are:
GATS: Fact and Fiction, World Trade Organization, Trade in Services Secretariat, Geneva, March 2001, available at http://www.wto.org , and
Open Services Markets Matter, OECD, Working Party of the Trade Committee, September 3, 2001, TD/TC/WP(2001)24/PART1/REV1.
Sinclair and Grieshaber-Otto (2002) op. cit. provide a critical analysis of many of the claims contained in these documents.

[3] As just one example, in a February 2001 opinion piece published in the *Guardian*, WTO Director General Michael Moore asserted that "GATS explicitly excludes services supplied by governments" – a statement that reading the GATS text shows to be untrue.
" Liberalization? Don't reject it just yet", Mike Moore, *Guardian*, 26 February 2001. Cited in Sinclair and Grieshaber-Otto, 2002. Also, see the discussion of the GATS governmental authority exclusion in Section 2.1.2

[4] Sinclair and Grieshaber-Otto, 2002. op. cit.

[5] See Section 3.1.4

[6] See Sections 2.1.2 and 3.4.1.
Note that Edison Schools asserts that "We ... compete for public school funding with existing public schools."
(Edison Schools Inc. (EDSN), We expect our market to become more competitive, Quarterly Report, February 14, 2002, op. cit.).

[7] The US could argue, for example, that differential subsidization amounts to a prohibited measure which has the effect of restricting "specific types of legal entit[ies]" through which a service is supplied (Article XVI(2)(e).

[8] This exclusion is considered above, initially in section 2.1.2.

[9] Among its horizontal limitations, the US lists "All Sectors: Subsidies[; Mode] 1) Unbound [Mode] 2) Unbound" in both the national treatment and market access categories.
(United States, Schedule of Specific Commitments, General Agreement on Trade in Services, 15 April 1994, GATS/SC/90.)

[10] This limitation, which immediately follows the public service limitation in Canada's schedule, reads: "Subsidies related to research and development – unbound".
(Canada, Schedule of Specific Commitments, GATS/SC/16, op. cit.).

[11] As previously noted, see Article XVI(2)(e).

[12] While the point requires closer examination, the same observation may also be true in the case of market access commitments.
Also, in addition to the points already noted in the text, citizens in other countries should note that this horizontal limitation appears to reflect Canada's view that *the supply of at*

least some public services is, in itself, is a violation of the GATS national treatment obligations.

13 Standard & Poor's Corp., the financial rating company, recently began offering, for a fee, state-wide cost-benefit analyses of schools and school districts. Michigan, Pennsylvania, Minnesota and Indiana are among states that reportedly have, or are considering, contracting with S&P for this purpose. William J. Cox, managing director of S&P's School Evaluation Services, predicts that within a decade, the service will have "a presence in every state".

In calculating its cost-benefit analyses, S&P reportedly measures a "performance cost index", which is derived from incorporating three kinds of student text scores, together with per-student spending, into an equation. The company then estimates how much additional per-student funding would increase, to a given proportion, the number of students passing state test scores. In light of the obvious complexities – including, for example, agreeing on an appropriate definition of academic success, and accounting for academic expenditures that are not geared to test scores — such services have yet to generate the controversy they probably warrant. (Gorman, Siobhan, EDUCATION: Standard & Poor's Goes to School, *National Journal*, July 28, 2001, available online to members at http://www.elibrary.ca).

14 16 The lone exception could be "school evaluation services"; one would expect the others to be classified in CPC 87404, 872, 87404 and 87, respectively.

15 Prominent GATS proponent Pierre Sauvé notes that "the GATS could play a useful role in helping achieve greater market openness ... [in] activities ancillary to education, such as quality assessment and testing..." (Pierre Sauvé, Trade Education and the GATS: What's in, what's out, what's all the fuss about?, op. cit., p. 28.)

16 This controversial LOTIS group has been active during the current round of GATS negotiations; see the first footnote of this chapter.

17 The LOTIS paper states:
"[T]he UK Government has said that there will be no offer in GATS in respect of *core* ... educational services; and other Governments are both able and likely to take a similar line.

It is much less obvious, however, that ancillary ... educational services should not be open to foreign competition..."
"The case for liberalising international trade in services", Liberalization of Trade in Services (LOTIS) Committee, International Financial Services, London, U.K., Circulated on the Global Services Network (GSN) listserv on May 15, 2002. The GSN website is http://www.globalservicesnetwork.com.

[18] This section draws heavily upon Sinclair (2000) and Sinclair and Grieshaber-Otto (2002), op. cit..

[19] Article VI:4, emphasis added.

[20] World Trade Organization, Working Party on Professional Services, "The Relevance of the Disciplines of the Agreements on Technical Barriers to Trade and on Import Licensing to Article VI.4 of the GATS," Note by the Secretariat, 11 September 1996 (S/WPPS/W/9). Cited in Sinclair and Grieshaber-Otto, 2002, op. cit..

[21] In a paper prepared for a recent OECD/US forum on trade in educational services, GATS proponent Pierre Sauvé emphasizes the importance of the GATS domestic regulation provisions:
"[T]he GATS could play a useful role ... in ensuring that regulatory measures in this area ... even while non-discriminatory in character, are not unduly burdensome or indeed disguised restrictions to trade and investment in the sector. The adoption of possible disciplines on domestic regulation ... and in particular the adoption of a necessity test ... could be important in this regard, though one cannot underestimate the political sensitivities that lie ahead in this area."
(Pierre Sauvé, *Trade, Education and the GATS*, op. cit., p. 28.)

[22] In sharp contrast to other clauses in Article VI, subsection 4 does not contain language that would limit its application to "sectors in which a Member has undertaken specific commitments".

[23] Sinclair and Grieshaber-Otto, 2002, op. cit..

[24] Public concerns about the policy implications of public-private partnerships under NAFTA and GATS was apparently central in the June 28, 2001 decision, by the Greater Vancouver Regional District, not to proceed with a proposal to establish a water filtration plant on a design-build-operate basis. (See "Water Design-Build-Operate Projects, memorandum from Water Committee Chair Marvin Hunt and Com-

missioner Johnny Carline to GVWD Board, June 28, 2001.) A critical review of relevant issues is contained in a legal opinion concerning the proposed project. (Shrybman, Steven, A legal opinion concerning the potential impact of international trade disciplines on proposals to establish a public-private partnership to design, build and operate a water filtration plant in the Seymour Reservoir, prepared for the Canadian Union of Public Employees, May 31, 2001.) Both documents are available from the authors. Many issues similar to those relating to water services could arise in education-related public-private partnerships. It is in this context that Canada's specific commitments on construction services, for example, could be of greatest relevance (see Section 2.3.2).

Chapter 5

[1] Canadian Knowledge Industry, DFAIT website: http://www.dfait-maeci.gc.ca/ics-cki/industry-e.asp.
According to DFAIT "The Canadian knowledge industry consists of public and private institutions, companies and organizations that provide primary, secondary, post-secondary, vocational, and corporate education and training or produce educational material, texts and software. Industry exports include:
- Sales of distance education programs and expertise
- Procurement of overseas corporate, government and group training contracts
- Procurement of International Financial Institution-funded education and training projects
- Recruitment of international students
- Procurement of foreign funding for research and development work
- Sales of printed and electronic educational materials including textbooks and CD-ROMs."

[2] Ibid..

[3] World Trade Organization, Council for Trade in Services, Special Session, Communication from Canada, Initial Canadian Negotiating Proposals, S/CSS/W/46, 14 March 2001, para. 7(i) and S/CSS/W/46/Corr.1, 23 March 2001.

4   Frequently asked questions about the GATS, Industry Canada website, http://www.strategis.ic.gc.ca/SSG/sk00100e.html#health , updated 25 May 2001.
5   The commercial education and training services industry, A discussion paper in preparation for the World Trade Organization General Agreement on Trade in Services (GATS) Negotiations, International Investment and Services Directorate, Industry Canada, available online from http://services2000.ic.gc.ca .
6   Frequently Asked Questions about the GATS, op. cit.
7   Hon. Pierre Pettigrew, quoted in: "B.C. worries trade talks will imperil health care", *Globe and Mail*, October 7, 1999.
8   Frequently asked questions about the GATS, op. cit..
9   Ibid..
10 Chen, Shenjie, Trade and Investment in Canada's Services Sector: Performance and Prospects, in *Trade Policy Research 2002*, edited by John M. Curtis and Dan Ciuriak, available online at http://www.dfait-maeci.gc.ca/eet/TPR_2002_e.pdf .
11 Ibid., p. 322.
12 Ibid., Table 26.
13 This is not restricted to education services, and — setting aside assessments of economic benefits — even basic trade information is lacking in many service sectors. "No country has ever constructed a data set to pull together a comprehensive picture of services trade through all four modes and across all sectors." (Ibid., p. 292.)
14 For example, in a recent presentation to the Canadian Teachers' Federation, federal officials reported:
"   Canadian commercial education/training interests and public institutions are active in the sale of educational expertise. *Few trade barriers have been reported.*" (emphasis added)
    GATS 2000 Negotiations and Education Services, Presentation to the Canadian Teachers' Federation, April 23, 2001, p. 15. Obtained through Access to Information Act Request No. A-2001-00038, p. 71.
15 It should be noted that these benefits are separate from those enjoyed by Canadian citizens. Also, the potential for such benefits to harm public service systems in other countries is generally overlooked. While this impact is beyond the scope

of this paper, it is an important aspect of GATS negotiations that warrants rigorous examination.

[16] Many of these concerns were outlined in the government's presentations to the Canadian Teachers' Federation and to the Council of Ministers of Education in April 2001.

[17] The relevant excerpt is as follows:
"Question 5: Canada will not negotiate its hospital services. Does that include not negotiating hospital based services such as janitorial services or food and laundry services? Answer 5: Let's keep clear that janitorial or food services are just that – they are not health services when provided in a hospital, just as they are not educational services when provided in schools."
Health Q&As, draft questions and answers prepared for presentation to federal minister for international trade on 9 March 2001, Obtained through Access to Information Act Request No. A-2001-00034, p. 106A.

[18] The Commercial Education and Training Services Industry, A discussion paper in preparation for the World Trade Organization General Agreement on Trade in Services (GATS) negotiations, Industry Canada, undated. (available at http://strategis.ic.gc.ca/SSG/sk00064e.html). This consultation paper also asks "Are there *certain areas* in your sector that you feel should not be included in international agreements? Why?" (emphasis added)

[19] Letter from International Trade Minister Pierre Pettigrew to Richard Epp, President of the University of Lethbridge Faculty Association, September 19, 2000, Obtained through Access to Information Act Request No. A-2001-00033, p. 197.

[20] Italics and underlining are added for emphasis and clarity in each of the quotations cited in this paragraph.

[21] As noted later, this statement, which appears to be broadly reassuring, may in fact be rather narrow.

[22] GATS 2000 Negotiations and Education Services, Presentation to the Canadian Teachers' Federation, April 23, 2001, p. 13. Obtained through Access to Information Act Request No. A-2001-00038, p. 69.

[23] GATS Negotiations and Education Services, briefing note prepared for meeting between federal officials and representatives of the Canadian Association of University Teachers

(CAUT), April 26, 2001. Obtained through Access to Information Act Request No. A-2001-00038, p. 128

24 "1. Currently the last sentence of the third paragraph on the page entitled 'GATS 2000 Negotiations' reads:
'In addition to pursuing these areas where Canada will be advancing an offensive agenda vis a vis other countries, the Government of Canada has made it clear that Canada's freedom to take action in key sectors, including health, *education* and culture will be upheld.'
This should be changed to read:
'...the Government of Canada has made it clear that Canada will ensure that it preserves its ability to adopt or maintain regulations, administrative practices or other measures in sectors such as health, *public education*, social services and culture.
WEB page Health Scrub, E-mail from federal officials Mark Crawford to Jake Vellinga, March 14, 2001. Obtained through Access to Information Act Request No. A-2001-00035, p. 28, (emphasis added in both excerpts).
It is interesting to speculate that these careful changes, made to material destined for the government's website, may not have been incorporated in material provided to the Minister in time for him to use in Oral Question Period the following week. At that time, in response to a question by Libby Davies, MP, Minister Pettigrew used the old message, which has since been discarded: "Some countries may decide to open their *education* system. ... This is not something Canada will do." (emphasis added) Available at http://www.parl.gc.ca/37/1/parlbus/chambus/house/debates/031 2001-03-19/ques031-E.htm .

25 Is Canada's public education system threatened? The GATS, Public Services, Health and Education, Services 2000 – GATS FAQs, Industry Canada website. (available at http://strategis.ic.gc.ca/SSG/sk00100e.html)

26 Concern about this lack of clarity is heightened by the government's confusing and contradictory assertions about the critical 'governmental authority' exclusion (see subsequent section).

27 Far from a mere quibble, the country's negotiating strategy should be based on a full recognition of the fundamental sig-

Perilous Lessons   181

28 nificance, to millions of Canadian citizens and to the economy, of education generally and of public education in particular. But can't bigger countries like the United States force us to negotiate our public services? The GATS, Public Services, Health and Education, Services 2000 – GATS FAQs, Industry Canada website. (available at http://strategis.ic.gc.ca/SSG/sk00100e.html)

29 Is Canada's public education system threatened?, Industry Canada website, op. cit.

30 Letter from International Trade Minister Pierre Pettigrew to Richard Epp, President of the University of Lethbridge Faculty Association, September 19, 2000, Obtained through Access to Information Act Request No. A-2001-00033, p. 197.

31 Note too, that this formulation is consistent with the notion, now under negotiation at the WTO, that while governments may be free to set their objectives, they should be obliged to achieve them through the least trade restrictive measures available. This in itself would constitute an important constraint on governments' regulatory ability.

32 See section 4.3.1

33 World Trade Organization, Council for Trade in Services, Communication from Canada, S/CSS/W/46 and S/CSS/W/46/Corr.1, op. cit..

34 Some of these issues have already been considered in Section 4.4.1 above, on Domestic Regulation negotiations; see also Sections 2.3.3 and 3.5.1.

35 Is Canada's public education system threatened?, Industry Canada website, op. cit.

36 For example, it is contained in material presented to the Canadian Teachers' Federation and the Council of Ministers of Education, "Bottom Line – 'Public education is not negotiable'". GATS 2000 Negotiations and Education Services, op. cit.

37 Hansard, Oral Question Period, April 24, 2001. In response to question by Libby Davies, M.P. Available at http://www.parl.gc.ca/37/1/parlbus/chambus/house/debates/047_2001-04-24/ques047-E.htm#LINK61

38 See Section 3.3.1 above.

39 The Canadian Oxford Dictionary defines "negotiate" as "confer with others in order to reach a compromise or agreement."

Canadian Oxford Dictionary, Don Mills, Ontario, Oxford University Press, 1998, p. 973.

[40] The Canadian government assertion that public education is "not negotiable" mirrors the government's statements during the FTA and NAFTA debates, when it was claimed that *water* was not covered in either treaty as it had not been on the negotiating table and did not come up in negotiations. More recently, the Canadian government has quietly acknowledged that many types of water are indeed covered by NAFTA; in fact, representatives have pointed to NAFTA coverage as a key impediment to the introduction of federal legislation to prohibit bulk water exports.

[41] GATS 2000 Negotiations and Education Services, Presentation to the Canadian Teachers' Federation, April 23, 2001, p. 15. Obtained through Access to Information Act Request No. A-2001-00038, p. 71.

Also, GATS 2000 Negotiations: Higher Education Services, Presentation to the Council of Ministers of Education, Canada, April 2, 2001, p. 16. Obtained through Access to Information Act Request No. A-2001-00038, p. 88.

[42] The Government's website states, for example:
"The GATS cannot be interpreted as requiring governments to privatize or to deregulate any service."
(Are critics correct in saying that, through the GATS negotiations, some countries are attempting to open up public services (health, public education, social services) for exploitation?, The GATS, Public Services, Health and Education, Services 2000 – GATS FAQs, Industry Canada website, op. cit.)

[43] See Sinclair and Grieshaber-Otto, op. cit..

[44] See Section 3.4.3 above.

[45] In response to question from Bill Blaikie, M.P. Available at http://www.parl.gc.ca/37/1/parlbus/chambus/house/debates/016_2001-02-19/ques016-E.htm#LINK25

[46] See Section 2.1.2.

[47] Some recent assertions by federal representatives appear to play down the significance of the exclusion. These claims avoid, in colloquial terms, putting all of the protective eggs in the 'governmental authority' basket. Instead, protection is claimed exist not only through the existence of the exclusion, but also through the lack of specific commitments in education services. This may be considered at once encouraging

and troubling. On the one hand, it may indicate that federal representatives now recognize the very limited, if any, protection the exclusion affords ... and the growing understanding among citizens worldwide of this fact. On the other hand, reaching to the lack of specific commitments as a form of protection is worrisome. The services that have not been committed are not excluded, or 'carved out', of the treaty. They are not protected in the way an excluded service would be – they merely haven't been subjected to the most onerous GATS rules. Citing non-committed services as a form of protection also seems an odd strategy for a government that appears to be prepared to make specific commitments in the sector – thereby losing important elements of the protection it purports to value.

The following are examples of representatives citing such 'two-prong' protection (italics and underlining are added in each example for emphasis):

"In my view, *the absence of commitments* by Canada in this sector, <u>coupled with</u> the current exclusion from the GATS of 'services supplied in the exercise of governmental authority', would ensure that Canadian authorities at all levels maintain the right to regulate the public education system, based on Canadian objectives and priorities."
Letter from International Trade Minister Pierre Pettigrew to Richard Epp, President of the University of Lethbridge Faculty Association, September 19, 2000, Obtained through Access to Information Act Request No. A-2001-00033, p. 197.

"Canada's ability to adopt or maintain regulations, administrative practices or other measures in public education is *preserved through the exclusion* of 'services supplied in the exercise of governmental authority' from the GATS, <u>coupled with</u> the absence of commitments regarding education."
GATS Negotiations and Education Services, briefing note prepared for meeting between federal officials and representatives of the Canadian Association of University Teachers (CAUT), April 26, 2001. Obtained through Access to Information Act Request No. A-2001-00038, p. 128.

48   "The Commercial Education and Training Services Industry", A discussion paper in preparation for the World Trade Organization General Agreement on Trade in Services (GATS) Negotiations, Industry Canada. (available at <u>http://</u>

strategis.ic.gc.ca/SSG/sk00064e.html) In each of the following quotations, italics and underlining is added for emphasis.

49   Ibid., Section V. Analysis of GATS Commitments Related to Education and Training,, para. 1.

50   Ibid., Section II. The Education and Training Industry, para. 2. It should be noted here that this paragraph itself seems to employ two different interpretations — one that the exclusion covers 'services provided by or receiving support from public authorities' the other that it covers education services 'provided by the State'. The entire paragraph reads as follows:

"Basic education, principally primary and secondary education, is often considered a social entitlement and, as a result, is often provided by (or with support from) public authorities. Such education services, provided by the State, are considered services 'supplied in the exercise of government (sic) authority' and thus are not covered by the GATS. The GATS covers only primary, secondary, tertiary/higher, adult, and other educational services supplied on a commercial basis where competition is allowed (subsequently referred to as commercial education and training services)."

In a slightly different context, it should also be noted that the document here dubiously equates "the State" with "public authorities".

51   Ibid., Canada Specifically ..., para. 1.

52   It will be recalled that Article I(3)(c) states that excluded services are those supplied "neither on a commercial basis, nor in competition with one or more service suppliers."

53   This statement is rendered more, not less, disturbing by the fact that it is prefaced with the bland observation that "Canada has a broad interpretation" of the exclusion, as it suggests officials are well aware that the statement is unsupportable.

54   Internal federal government note, dated November 12, 1999, prepared in response to the Globe and Mail article entitled "Education: Training to be a hot issue in WTO" that appeared the previous day. Obtained through Access to Information Act Request No. A-2001-00033, p. 154.

Chapter 6

[1] GATS article XIX:3.
[2] WTO Council for Trade in Services, *Communication from Cuba, Dominican Republic, Haiti, India, Kenya, Pakistan, Peru, Uganda, Venezuela and Zimbabwe*, 9 October 2001,S/CSS/WII4.
[3] Sinclair, 2000, op. cit., pp. 13-14.